Please renew/return this item by the last date shown.

So that your telephone call is charged at local rate,
please call the numbers as set out below:

From Area codes 01923 or 0208:	From the rest of Herts:
Renewals: 01923 471373	01438 737373
Enquiries: 01923 471333	01438 737333
Minicom: 01923 471599	01438 737599

L32b   Checked 15/9/11

1 8 AUG 200

8 SEPT 2005
   9/12

L32a

D1330893

ZEST FOR LIFE

ZEST FOR LIFE

Mary Bagot Stack

and the League of Health and Beauty

by Prunella Stack

PETER OWEN · LONDON

ISBN 0 7206 0697 7

PETER OWEN PUBLISHERS
73 Kenway Road London SW5 0RE

First published in Great Britain 1988
© Prunella Stack 1988

Photoset by Ann Buchan (Typesetters), Middlesex
Printed and bound in Great Britain
by A. Wheaton & Co. Ltd, Exeter

To my granddaughters
Saba and Mara Douglas-Hamilton,
the fourth generation

Preface

This is the story of the life and work of one woman – my mother. Much of it I know from my own experience; some of it from what I have read or been told; the rest from the intuition born of love.

My mother was a visionary who turned her dreams into realities. I can write about this as the one who was closest to her, for she brought me up on her pioneer views of health and put them into practice in our daily lives. In 1930 she founded a movement, the Women's League of Health and Beauty, which was to change the outlook of a whole generation of women. The ideas about healthy living which it propagated at the time were widely disseminated over the years and have now become accepted wisdom.

> The intellect of man is forced to choose
> Perfection of the life or of the work.
>
> (Yeats)

Part One of this book tells my mother's story up to the early years of the 1914–18 war when my father was killed. Perfection of the life ended for her then and she turned to perfection of the work. Part Two describes the way in which she achieved this and how, after her untimely death, I carried on her movement. With the help of the teachers she had trained it became spectacularly successful, spreading to countries abroad, surviving the war years, and then attracting new teachers and new members who carried it forward through changing conditions to the different emphasis of today.

Preface

In some ways my mother's life and mine followed the same pattern. We both knew loss and grief as well as success and fulfilment. In writing about her experiences I have been able to draw on my own. She triumphed over her ordeals and preserved her inspiration. It lives on for many thousands of women to whom her work has brought increased health and happiness.

I like to think that this work, to which my mother dedicated her life, has the self-renewing quality of a phoenix, so that whatever happens to its changing outer form her inner vision for it will endure.

Contents

Illustrations

Acknowledgements

I would like to express my grateful thanks to my husband Brian
for giving me the idea for this book and for critical help; my
cousins Hugo and Peter Luttman-Johnson, Christopher
Seton-Watson and Cinderella Child for family papers and
photographs; Marjorie Duncombe for memories of my mother;
Vicki Barter and Kathryn Wilson for typing the manuscript; and
my editors Beatrice Musgrave and Antonia Owen for their
sensitive suggestions and advice.

P.S.

PART ONE

1

The Salmon Leap

My mother's story starts in Dublin in the 1880s. She was born in that city of contrasts where wide streets ended in views of distant mountains, where tenement houses jostled with Georgian façades, where the River Liffey flowed under ornate bridges to the port, the ships and the sea. It seemed like a country town. But it was also a capital city – a city adorned with graceful eighteenth-century public buildings which included a castle and a Viceregal Lodge, where Queen Victoria's Viceroy lived and ruled.

Across the water lay England, centre of an empire which circled the globe. Each continent contained dedicated men, sworn to extend and preserve British rule. White, brown and black people swelled the total of Victoria's subjects. And the number of those subjects increased every day.

In Ireland, the Protestant Anglo-Irish ruling class served and supported this empire. But among the Catholic Irish people rebellion festered. Famine, emigration and deprivation had halved their numbers. Yet still the hope for an independent Ireland remained.

Also in Dublin at this time were a group of young men – the poet Yeats among them – who were interested in reviving the Irish language and ancient Irish traditions. They believed that through these things, rather than through politics, a new sense of national pride would be born.

Early in the morning the life of the city began. Shops opened

15

their shutters, hawkers cried their wares, and horses trotted down the streets dragging their carts behind them.

On 12 June 1883, in one of the tall Georgian houses, my grandmother lay in labour. She had been brought to bed with her fourth child. The house was hushed. Even the other children, two boys and a girl, remained quiet. Her husband and her doctor waited as the hours passed.

At last when the sun was at its zenith at midday, her baby was born – a girl with a crop of black hair and blue eyes. She was christened Mary Meta but was always known to her family and friends as Mollie.

Her parents were Theodore and Charlotte Stack, Protestants from the North. Their home town was Omagh in County Tyrone where they both grew up, learning to respect the Protestant virtues of hard work, probity and self-help. After their marriage in 1873 they moved to Dublin. Theodore had recently returned from America where he had taken an honours degree in dentistry at Harvard University. A previous bout of rheumatic fever had affected his heart and his hearing and forced him to abandon his profession as a doctor. He decided to change careers, came to Dublin and established a dental practice in a large Georgian house in fashionable Merrion Square. There his eldest son George was born in 1879. A second son, Harry, followed one year later, and then came a daughter, Nan, in 1882. So Mollie's first memories were of her brothers and her sister, strong personalities among whom she had to fight for her place.

Mollie always loved Dublin. As a child she knew its pavements, crossed by lines on which she tried not to step, the iron railings of the square garden along which she drew a finger as she trotted beside them, and the low wall where she balanced for a few daring strides.

St Stephen's Green was the setting for her daily walks. It contained what seemed to her immense areas of grass, but also bushes where she and her sister Nan could make houses too small for grown-ups, but just the right size for the fairy visitors they expected. Her brothers sailed boats on the lake. Mallards swam to the edge of it and the little girls fed them with crumbs, matching the beady regard of the birds' eyes with their own interested stares.

In the winter, dressed in warm woolly coats, fur hats and muffs, gaiters and button boots, they returned home as it was getting dark. The austere façades of the Merrion Square houses rose like cliffs of brick above them, broken only by a few delicate wrought-iron balconies, where sometimes they were allowed to stand. Behind their backs lay the gardens of the square. Witches and wild beasts might be lurking there among the shadows. The little girls ran up the wide stone steps to the front doorway of their house and saw the glow of its lantern shining through the glass fanlight. The door opened and welcomed them to safety just in time.

Mollie and Nan resembled each other with their rounded faces, chubby cheeks and straight noses, but Mollie had her father's deep-set green eyes and dark curly hair, parted in the middle. She also inherited several traits of his adventurous character.

Theodore had swept his wife Charlotte off her feet during their courtship. She thought of him as a kind of meteor who had flashed across her horizon, exciting and disturbing her with his urgent vitality. But her mother had seen him differently. Although Theodore was already immersed in his profession as a doctor, healing his patients as much by the force of his personality as by his medical knowledge, his connections were not aristocratic enough for Charlotte's mother. She wanted her only daughter to marry someone akin to her own county family, the Blakes of Castlegrove in County Galway. Charlotte's father, Henry Thompson, Medical Superintendent of the Omagh Infirmary, was in favour of the match, but nevertheless the couple had to wait for several years until Theodore's persistance and Charlotte's fidelity prevailed.

From the first, Mollie formed a close and special bond with her father, and as she grew older his knowledge of medicine and the healing arts interested her more and more.

In 1886 another daughter, Charlotte, was born, followed two years later by the last child of the family, Norah. By the end of that decade Mollie's elder brothers George and Harry were at school and Nan and Mollie had started lessons. Theodore was increasingly busy during the week, but Saturdays and Sundays

were kept for his family. On those evenings they all assembled
in the drawing-room of the Merrion Square house, a circle of
chairs drawn up round the fire. Mollie sat on the floor leaning
against her father's knee and listened to his voice as he read
aloud. Sometimes he chose poems from a collection of Yeats's
which had just been published. One of Mollie's favourites was
'The Stolen Child' with its haunting refrain:

> Come away, O human child!
> To the waters and the wild
> With a faery, hand in hand,
> For the world's more full of weeping than you can
>   understand.

Her brothers preferred tales of battles from Ireland's heroic
age. But whatever was being read they all listened carefully to
their father's resonant voice; and in future years Mollie would
remember these moments when her vital, vigorous family
seemed to be united and at peace.

Mollie's life continued uneventfully with its daily lessons and
walks, its Sunday church-going, its skirmishes with her
brothers and sisters, and its weekend activities with her father,
until she was eight years old. Then suddenly everything
changed. She became gravely ill. She contracted peritonitis and
the infection spread so rapidly that her life was in danger.

She lay on the small white bed in her room, the house silent
as at her birth, her eyes closed and her parents beside her.
Charlotte had watched through her fever and pain, and
Theodore had summoned a specialist to attend her. Now all
they could do was to wait for the crisis of her illness to be
resolved.

'She's exhausted,' Charlotte whispered. 'Her strength has
gone.'

Theodore leant forward. He took one of Mollie's hands in
both his own and began to stroke it very gently, staring with all
his force into her face. His whole being seemed concentrated
into one fine point, a ray directed to penetrate the
consciousness of his child.

Mollie lay unstirring. During her fever everything had
seemed needle sharp, the shapes of shadowy figures magnified

into giants, the smallest sounds grating and hurting her head. Now, with the fever gone, she felt hollow and completely passive. She was drifting further and further away from all she had known, drifting on a tide which carried her unresisting down a dark stream.

'Mollie.' Theodore's voice spoke softly as he leant closer to the bed. Mollie heard it in her unconscious and felt the presence of his hand. Something, someone was calling her back. But she did not want to come. It was so much easier to drift on.

'Mollie!' The voice sounded again and a wave of warm strength coursed into her body from that firm clasped hand. The darkness of the stream lightened, and now she was rising from the depths of a deep well into some kind of light. . . .

'*Mollie.*' Painfully she opened her eyes. They focused, and she was aware of someone leaning over her. It was her father. Tears gathered in her eyes. 'Oh, Pappy,' she whispered. That was the turning-point of her illness. And in after-years she was convinced that no one but her father could have 'brought her back from the dead'.

To convalesce, Mollie's mother took her to Mullaghmore, Theodore's family home near Omagh. Three generations of her father's family had lived in this small manor house and he had been born and brought up there.

The Stacks had owned two or three hundred acres of land around Mullaghmore, and the river as far as a waterfall called the Salmon Leap. Mollie and her mother walked up to it through woods of silver birch, where sunlight filtered through the branches and moss grew underfoot.

At the fall, below the cascading water lay a deep pool, a transparent peaty-brown coated with ripples and drifts of white foam. Here the salmon gathered in the spring, lying just under the surface in great numbers, biding their time and summoning their strength until the moment came for the flashing leap that would carry them to the top of the rock face.

'And if they don't get there the first time,' said Charlotte, 'if they fall back into the pool, they try again and again. They've swum all the way up the river from the sea and they must finish their journey to their breeding places.'

Mollie thought of the small boy who had been her father. He must often have watched the salmon flashing out of the water, risking death against the rock, leaping up and up until they reached the still safe water above the fall. She would tell him she had seen the place.

Behind Mullaghmore House lay farm buildings and stables where the pony who drew the trap was looked after by Dan the gardener, who was also a groom. He set Mollie on the pony and led her through the grounds, telling her stories of the old house. In these peaceful surroundings she grew stronger each day and by the time a month had passed she was ready to go back to Dublin, her health restored.

The claims of education began to separate the family. First George and then Nan went to English schools, their Anglo-Irish parents believing that a better education could be had overseas. Harry, the second son, attended Galway Grammar School; and Mollie, Charlotte and Norah were put down for Alexandra School in Dublin. Mollie went there in September 1893 when she was ten years old.

Her headmistress, Dr Isabella Mulvaney, had been a scholarship pupil at Alexandra College and became headmistress of the school in 1880. She encouraged a high academic standard and expected the girls to work very hard. Places were allotted each week as a result of written tests. The subjects studied were arithmetic, English, writing, English history, ancient and modern history, geography, French, needlework and elementary mathematics. Mollie also took music, and later German. She was intelligent and could apply herself well, but she needed to have a strong motive to stretch herself to the limit. The dreamy side of her nature was liable to take command, and she preferred subjects like English, writing and history where she could lose herself in speculation or self-expression without too much mental effort.

At the end of the term reports were presented to parents. Theodore's children were apprehensive of this moment and their subsequent interview with their father. He demanded good results in all subjects.

'Why aren't you first in your class?' he would thunder,

drawing his thick eyebrows together and slapping the offending report on the table. Excuses of disliked teachers, difficult subjects or lack of understanding were given short shrift. 'What you need, Mollie, is concentration. You live too much in the past or the future, or in dreams. The present is only here for a second – not that – then it is past, and the future quickly becomes the present and races into the past again. The *present* – brace yourself and concentrate on the present, and draw the utmost from each second.'

Mollie tried to explain that she hated arithmetic and mathematics and did not want to live in the present while they were being taught, or to concentrate on them.

'All the more reason why you should,' Theodore declared. 'You must set yourself at the things you don't like, not run away from them.' He paused, looking at her tearful face. 'Listen. Do you remember telling me about those salmon leaping the waterfall at Mullaghmore? Some of them managed to do it the first time. Others had to try over and over again. Your dislike of arithmetic is like the salmon being swept against the rocks and falling back again. But they don't heed the knocks. They never give up. They go on and on until they succeed. So must you.'

A picture of the cool river and the silver fish leaping out of it rose before Mollie's eyes. How she wished she was there, instead of standing beside the table in her father's study! He seemed a stranger when he was in this mood. 'I will try, Pappy,' she murmured, as he dismissed her and turned to the papers on his desk.

Mollie took his homily to heart. At the end of the next term she was able to produce a report in which she received the comment 'excellent' for thirteen subjects and 'very good' for the remaining two. And thereafter she won a scholarship each year in the public examinations for which the pupils of Alexandra School entered every summer.

Mollie went to Alexandra School at the same time as the foundations were being laid for an Irish literary revival in Dublin. The cause of Irish Home Rule had failed with the rejection of Gladstone's bill by the House of Lords in 1893 and the subsequent defeat of his Liberal Party in 1895. Irish independence appeared to be indefinitely postponed. And yet, at that time, a new sense of pride was stirring among a number of Irish writers, an urge to celebrate their national language and culture.

For many generations, they said, Ireland had been a poor copy of England, bound by alien customs, speaking a foreign tongue. Now, she must return to her ancient traditions. She must retrieve her Irishness, discover her roots, learn and translate the poems of the Celtic bards which were still spoken in the country districts, preserve the Gaelic language and encourage its use. There was urgency in the task, because the old traditions and language were already dying away.

In 1893, Douglas Hyde, a Protestant and a brilliant scholar of Trinity College, founded the Gaelic League whose aim was 'to keep the Irish language spoken in Ireland'. It was an immediate success. Branches were established in towns and villages all over the country and Irish language folklore, music and dancing were widely taught. Irish festivals were organized and Gaelic books and pamphlets published. Within ten years membership of the Gaelic League had grown to 50,000; financial assistance even came from America, home of so many Irish emigrants.

This was also the year that Douglas Hyde published his *Love Songs of Connacht*, a collection of Gaelic poetry which he had gathered from peasants in the west of Ireland and from old manuscripts. Hyde, himself a poet, was able to render in English the unique quality of the Gaelic rhythm and syntax, something which had never been done before. Mollie learnt the poems at school and remembered them for the rest of her life.

Yeats, another pioneer of the movement, met Hyde while he was at Trinity College, and Hyde's insight into Gaelic culture influenced Yeats profoundly. It confirmed what he had already learnt from the Catholic Fenian John O'Leary, who believed that an Irish political revolution could never succeed without a cultural revival.

Yeats and his fellow founders of the Irish literary revival – Hyde, Synge and Lady Gregory – were all Protestants, although they addressed themselves to the main mass of Irish Catholic people. But most of the Protestants of Trinity College held a different view; they rejected the possibility of a purely

Irish culture. The Trinity establishment had close links with Oxford and Cambridge across the water and with the Viceregal Lodge in Dublin. Their traditions were of English origin.

Theodore was a graduate of Trinity. It was where his forebears had been educated. He loved Yeats's poetry and appreciated the vital influence of the Irish literary renaissance. Yet he chose to educate his daughters at Alexandra School and Alexandra College, both training grounds for Protestant girls comparable to Trinity, with which they had close connections.

Theodore was approaching the apex of his career. He was one of the founders of the School of Dentistry in Ireland and had been Dean since 1891. His own private practice flourished in the house in Merrion Square, but the rest of his time was spent teaching dental students and giving treatment to poor patients in inadequate premises which were totally unsuitable. The necessity for a well-equipped, central dental hospital in Dublin, where the School of Dentistry could be permanently housed, became paramount.

Theodore realized this and gave himself to the project with all his energy and idealism. It dominated his thoughts and actions for years. His enthusiasm spilled over to his family. Charlotte undertook to raise money for the hospital, and organized a huge Venetian Fête which secured the final sum necessary to start building. By 1895 the Dental Hospital was completed. It had an impressive opening. The prefix *Royal* was added to its title, and a portrait of Theodore by Walter Osborne, RA, was placed on its walls, with this inscription:

Richard Theodore Stack
MD FRCSI DMD Harvard

One of the Founders of the Dental Hospital
and School of Dentistry in Ireland.

This portrait has been placed in the
Hospital during his period of office as Dean
of the School by his Colleagues, to mark their

recognition of his services to the Dental
Profession in Ireland.

The new Royal Dental Hospital in Lincoln Place adjoined
Trinity College. From his office Theodore could look out over
the quadrangles, the spacious avenues, the flights of steps and
the dignified buildings that constituted this centre of
Anglo-Irish education. His younger son, Harry, went to
Trinity a year later in 1896, aged sixteen. Harry had benefited
from the standards of excellence imposed on the family by his
father and was accepted, although very young, to study for a
medical degree. George, two years older, was already at the
Royal Engineers' Academy at Woolwich in England, training
to be a military engineer.

With Nan's absence in school at Eastbourne, Mollie turned
for companionship to her younger sister Charlotte, aged eleven,
who was now at school with her. Charlotte's name had been
abbreviated to Charlie, a rather tomboyish appellation for such
a sensitive, withdrawn and highly-strung child. Charlie found
Mollie a much more boisterous and challenging companion
than her former playmate Norah, the youngest of the family,
who was a delicate little girl requiring her mother's constant
care.

Charlie tried to keep up with Mollie, but she possessed
certain high principles and ideals that tended to conflict with
the hurly-burly of school and family life, resulting in a constant
inner nervous tension. She was clever and conscientious and
she liked school; but her reserve prevented her from making
friends as quickly as the outgoing Mollie and her sensitive
nature dreaded her father's brusque end-of-term inquiries
about her progress.

One day Charlie came home from school alone and opened
the front door. The light in the hall was dim, but she could
clearly see a body stretched out on the floor. She wanted to
scream. Then she realized it was her father. He was lying on his
back on the floor of the hall, his eyes closed and his breathing
deep. She ran to his side and knelt beside him.

'Pappy, what is it?' she called, rigid with fear.

He opened his eyes and smiled. 'Don't worry, Charlie dear,'
he said. 'I was just having a wee rest. My heart is a bit tired.'

Charlie laughed with relief, but at the same time a warning bell sounded in her mind. Her father knew his heart was weak, and so he was resting. But why on the floor of the hall?

Theodore had built an extension at the back of the house, primarily to accommodate his increased practice. He also included in it a large room with a stage where his children could produce plays. He threw himself into this project with his usual fervour and decided to open it with a series of *tableaux vivants* in honour of Queen Victoria's Diamond Jubilee on 22 June 1897.

The Jubilee was being received with mixed feelings in Dublin. The Anglo-Irish were determined to support a patriotic parade in honour of their Queen, but the Nationalists, the Fenians and many others bitterly resented what they considered to be a public display of English domination.

Theodore decided to show where he stood. He marshalled his forces. George got leave from the Military Academy in Woolwich to return home and Nan was granted a long weekend from her school in Eastbourne. The younger children painted scenery, while their mother stitched costumes and Theodore strode about issuing instructions. He had thought out a number of scenes depicting dramatic moments in the history of the Empire, and his passion and enthusiasm were such that his children were induced to portray them with every resource they possessed. Charlie took part only under great pressure. She firmly refused any solo parts, but these were gladly accepted by George, Harry and Mollie.

Theodore's new room was crowded with friends and relations on the evening of the Jubilee. The velvet curtains in front of the stage parted slowly and the first tableau was disclosed – Mollie, dressed as an Irish colleen, saying an affectionate farewell to George, the young soldier, who was setting out to conquer distant lands. Nan sang the accompaniment.

> Oh! ne'er shall I forget the night
> The stars were bright above me,
> And gently lent their silvery light
> When first she vow'd to love me.
> But now I'm bound to soldier camp,
> Kind heaven, then pray guide me

And bring me safely back again
To the girl I left behind me.

To dutiful applause, the curtains creaked shut again, and
after a hectic interval backstage the next tableau appeared.
This involved the whole family, who were shown in the process
of landing on a distant foreign shore. Norah, the smallest, was
carried in George's arms; Nan, his young wife, held an
unwilling and retiring Charlie by the hand; Mollie, one hand
shading her eyes, gazed into the distance; while Harry, weighed
down with luggage, stepped manfully forward. Remembering
their father's instructions they all wore expressions of extreme
determination.

Scene followed scene, the children enjoying themselves
increasingly, until the evening ended with the waving of Union
Jacks and the singing of 'God Save the Queen'. Looking at her
father's face, Charlie saw it flushed, triumphant, a spot of
bright colour on each cheekbone. She noticed beads of sweat on
his forehead and once again an anxious pang contracted her
heart.

Meanwhile, outside in the streets of Dublin, a very different
celebration was taking place. An aggressive crowd had
gathered and was marching towards the City Hall, singing
nationalist slogans, smashing shop windows and fighting with
the police. They carried a black flag which they succeeded in
hoisting at half-mast above the City Hall. This procession
was followed later by another bearing a draped coffin covered
with skull-and-crossbones flags. It marched towards the
castle accompanied by the beat of a muffled drum. One of the
banners which it displayed bore the inscription *Starved to
Death*.

Theodore continued to drive himself in all aspects of his life. He
was now earning about £6,000 a year, a large sum for those
days, but he was spending it too – on the extension of his house,
on projects for the hospital, on education for his children.
Although still comparatively young – he was only forty-nine –
his health had never been robust and the constant strain of his
activities wore him out. In December 1897 he had a severe

stroke and lost his ability to speak and the use of his right leg and right arm.

The family assembled; this time in grief and bewilderment. His children could not believe that such a tragedy could befall their father. Silent, unmoving, he sat in his wheelchair, his mind as clear as ever but with no means of communication.

His income ceased. Theodore had never been able to save money, and when all the debts and liabilities were paid the family was badly off. They moved from Merrion Square to a house in Blackrock, a suburb of Dublin, and there Theodore started the long process of rehabilitation. He taught himself to write with his left hand, and then to speak, to begin with in a series of indistinct grunts.

For three years he had an attack every fortnight. He would mutter to himself and then suffer a mild epileptic fit. All the children, even the youngest, knew what to do: they had to put a spoon in his mouth to prevent him from biting his tongue. Gradually he got better. His valiant spirit revived and he fought his disability with his old determination. But now *he* was the dependant one who must be cared for and cherished. Mollie continued her school and home life, outwardly as before, but inwardly something important had happened to her. Suddenly she had grown up.

2

Taking Wing

On a June day in 1898 Mollie walked along the beach at Blackrock. The tide was out and sand gleamed under the early summer sunshine. On the horizon the hill of Howth stretched in a long curve to make the northern boundary of Dublin Bay. Beyond lay the open sea.

Mollie walked slowly. She had taken off her shoes and stockings to let the sand run through her toes. Her head, too, was bare; her hat swung in her hand. The wind lifted her long dark hair as she turned her gaze from the sea to the terrace of early Victorian houses above the shore.

Each of these houses had three storeys, a small front garden and a flight of steps leading to a painted front door. Above the two centre houses a pediment had been built on which was inscribed *Idrone-sur-Mer*. Between the houses and the shore ran a narrow road and then, in a deep cutting, a railway which connected Blackrock to Dublin. Early each morning Mollie and her sisters caught the train to school, travelling back again in the late afternoon. They would dash out of the house towards the station, running wildly up the road, hair and satchels flying; if they were late, the guard delayed the train until they arrived. Norah now attended school along with Mollie and Charlie, bringing up the rear and crying shrilly, 'Wait for me!'

Their father would watch the three of them from his seat by the bay window of the drawing-room on the first floor of the house. Thinking of him sitting there, Mollie tried to imagine the silent lonely world he now inhabited, so different from his former busy life. He often grew irritable when she could not understand him, yet he valued her company more than anyone else's. She looked again at the terrace of houses, found number 14, and lifting her arm high above her head waved her hat in case he could see her. Then turning her back on the houses, she ran down to the water's edge. The tide was on the turn, pushing transparent ripples up the shore. Mollie lifted her skirts and waded in.

Further up the coast was the port of Kingstown, from which the mail-boats sailed to England. At this time of day one was usually pulling out of the harbour, turning in a wide curve and making its way to the ocean. Mollie gazed across the water and spotted the ship, its white funnel gleaming, waves churning in its wake. This was what she had come to see. She began to day-dream.

One day, she told herself, *she* would go to England, as George and Nan had done. She would be on that ship, standing by the rail, watching the coast of Ireland fade away – school over, exams passed, grown up at last.

Smiling to herself, she flung both arms above her head and waved to the ship with all her might. The incoming tide drenched the hem of her skirt, but she was oblivious of this. And the steamer sailed deliberately on, out into the Irish sea.

Nan had left her school in Eastbourne after her father's stroke and come back home. Now she was studying singing in Dublin. She and Mollie had long talks together in the room they shared at the top of the house.

'What is it really like in England?' Mollie asked her one evening, curled up on a bed while her sister sat in a chair by the window.

'Very different from here.' Nan withdrew her gaze from the sea and looked at Mollie. 'The English have so much confidence. They think they're the greatest nation of the world and that makes them superior.'

'I don't think I'd like that.'

'You'd get used to it. They admire Irish talent and humour. They think we're a wild lot. Of course they don't differentiate between Catholics and Protestants. They lump us all together. Most of the best writers in London are Irish – Bernard Shaw,

Oscar Wilde, George Moore. And some of the best teaching of art, music and drama is there.'

'Is that why you want to go back?'

'Why, yes. I'd like to study singing there and in Paris. I'd love to be an opera singer! I couldn't learn here, not to a high enough standard. I could only hope to succeed if I went back.'

'You will, you will. I'm sure you will!' Mollie's eyes shone as she gazed at her sister.

'I don't know. It's so difficult now with Pappy so ill, and Mammy having to manage on so little money. You know, we'll all have to be breadwinners now. We must train for careers, so that we can earn money. But my training will be so long and so expensive. I don't see how they can afford it.'

'You must believe in yourself, like those superior English,' Mollie laughed. 'You're lucky to have finished with school. I've still got years of it ahead.'

'Well, you must work hard and be top of your exams. You can, Mollie, if you try. Then your turn will come.'

Mollie stirred restlessly at the thought of exams. She rose from the bed and came to stand beside her sister. Together they listened to the splash of the waves and watched the lights of Howth appear like pinpricks out of the darkness.

'It's beautiful here,' Mollie said. 'I'd miss it right enough if I left. I don't think the English understand the Irish.' Her jaw set in a firm line like her father's. 'But one day I'll go there and make them understand *me!*'

Mollie was starting her last year at Alexandra School before moving up to the college. She was used to working hard at her lessons, but this year called for a special effort. For some reason she had missed having Latin tuition and now she had to cram several years' work into one. Her teacher wanted her to enter for the Jellicoe Memorial Latin Prize at the end of the year. Girls at Alexandra School were taught Latin, in spite of the opinion in some quarters that they would be better occupied studying household management or child-care; this enabled them to sit for the Trinity examinations on the same footing as their male contemporaries.

Mollie knew how delighted her father would be if she managed to win the Latin prize, so she initiated a strict regime. Each night she set her alarm clock for 5.45 a.m. When it rang, her first impulse was to reach out her hand and throw it across the room. But it had done its job. She was awake. She slipped on her dressing-gown, picked up the clock, set its battered face on her desk and studied for two hours while the rest of the household slept.

In later life she would remember those early morning hours; the first birds singing, the first beams of light striking the Howth peninsula, and then the unexpected illumination of day when she raised her abstracted eyes from the page.

She also had to fit violin practice into her busy day. This was a new skill she was acquiring. It provided a welcome contrast from Latin, but required precious time.

In the late summer of 1899 Mollie sat the Latin examination and in September she heard the result. She had won the prize and was awarded £5. Now she would move up to the college. Her father's beaming face showed his approval, and her mother gave her a small ring with a moonstone, which was her birth-stone.

Alexandra College was flourishing under its far-sighted principal, Miss H. M. White. Housed in a number of buildings in Earlsfort Terrace, it possessed well-laid-out gardens and a large, circular, newly built hall – the Jellicoe Hall – where plays, assemblies and prize-givings could be held. The 'lady lecturers' of the staff were all graduates who taught their classes in impressive black academic gowns worn over white blouses with bow-ties. Lecturers from Trinity College also instructed the students and the Provost of Trinity was on the council.

Miss White had been to Alexandra College as a girl, and then to Newnham College in Cambridge. She was convinced of the right of women to have equal educational opportunities with men and thereafter careers. She could point to the success of her own college, where girls achieved a high academic standard but also engaged in a number of other activities.

For Mollie, life at the college widened her horizons considerably. She still worked very hard, but now she was treated less as a schoolgirl and more as a student. She joined the Hockey Club, playing in a long black skirt and a white blouse with a stiff collar, leg-o'-mutton sleeves and a tie. She cycled through the countryside with the Alexandra Cycling Club; and she listened to lectures on the history of painting, on archaeology, and on aspects of Irish civilization. Douglas Hyde came and discussed the Gaelic revival and the Gaelic League, inspiring such enthusiasm that classes in Irish were later introduced.

Mollie began to realize that although Ireland seemed to be divided into two nations there were bridges across the chasm – bridges of song, poetry, art. Both sides shared a love for the island's beauty, both felt themselves to be essentially Irish and distinct from any other people elsewhere. Lessons in Irish history made Mollie proud of her heritage; she began to understand why some of her countrymen wished to defend it with their lives.

> Know that I would accounted be
> True brother of a company
> That sang, to sweeten Ireland's wrong. . . .

Yeats's lines rang through her head with a sense of identification.

In April 1900, when Mollie had been at Alexandra College for two terms, Queen Victoria visited Dublin. The purpose of her visit was to thank the Irish troops who had fought in the Boer War. The Inniskillings, the Connaught Rangers, the Dublin Fusiliers and the Royal Irish Fusiliers had all served in South Africa and received heavy casualties.

Crowds lined the streets to watch the aged Queen pass, Mollie and her family among them. The old lady, in the last months of her life, was dressed as usual in deep mourning and so hunched in her carriage that she was unable to acknowledge the greetings of the crowd. Her reception was friendly, in spite of the fact that large sections of Irish opinion violently disapproved of her visit.

Kinship with the Boers who were struggling in South Africa against the might of the British Empire was strongly felt by many Irishmen, as well as resentment at England's neglect of Ireland during Victoria's reign. She was known as the Famine Queen. Nevertheless she was cheered as she drove to Phoenix Park; and Mollie, only dimly aware of the unspoken tensions in the crowd, loyally waved her Union Jack and tried not to feel disappointed at the plainness of the diminutive old lady who her brothers told her represented the greatest empire in the world.

The following year, in 1901, Harry, the youngest of the two, went to South Africa. He had gained his BA at Trinity and qualified as a doctor at the age of twenty-one – one of the youngest graduates to do so. He then volunteered to join a medical unit attached to an Irish regiment and departed overseas. Family loyalties consolidated around this gesture. Any doubts Theodore, or Mollie herself, might have had about the justice of the war were stifled for Harry's sake. They all felt a need to support him and be proud of his adventurous action. He served unharmed until the war ended in May 1902, and then returned to Trinity to take his final degree.

The high academic standards of Alexandra College kept Mollie working at full pitch. She fulfilled their demands and did well. She also joined the sports and social events and tried to experience everything the college had to offer. Her mother, watching this whole-hearted involvement, hoped she would not overstrain herself. Her father, gradually recovering his lost power of speech, used it to encourage her to further effort. But Mollie had worked too hard. When she was seventeen the strain showed itself in an attack of St Vitus' Dance, and this was followed by a more severe illness, rheumatic fever. Her body grew emaciated and listless as she fought the disease. Her exceptional vitality was eclipsed; all she could do was lie in her bed, enduring the pain, looking out from her window over the sea, watching the changing skies. She was living in a kind of limbo. The crisis of the illness passed and gradually she began to recover. However, she was still subject to attacks of rheumatism. The doctors insisted that she must lead an easy life for a year or two and give up her studies at Alexandra College, although she could continue some of them at home. Theodore had needed a professional nurse for the first years of his illness. Now that period was over and Mollie could take the nurse's place as his constant companion. So it was decreed that Mollie should remain at home and postpone her chance of training for a degree or career.

This was a deep disappointment for her and it was emphasized by the fact that Nan now had her chance to go abroad. Theodore's younger sister Mary and her husband Willy Geoghegan – a director of Guiness's Brewery and a rich man – offered to take Nan to London and then Paris and to pay for her singing training there.

Mollie suppressed the pangs of envy when she heard the news and flung her arms round her sister.

'Oh, Nan, I'm so happy for you,' she said. 'It's what you've always wanted. I'll miss you terribly.'

Nan consoled her, saying that her turn would come, but Mollie could foresee no future but that of caring for her mother and father. Alexandra College had sparked in her the desire for a career in the outside world and, although she did not yet know what form it would take, she was confident she could find creative work of her own choice if she was given the opportunity. Now all that must be set aside. Sadly she watched her sister leave and then set about helping her mother move with the family to a new house – one owned by the Geoghegans and lent to the Stacks indefinitely to tide them over the hard financial times they were experiencing.

This house, in an adjacent suburb called Foxrock, was a large one which stood in its own garden of flowering shrubs and had a view of the Wicklow mountains instead of the sea. It contained ample space for Mollie, her two schoolgirl sisters and the friends they began to attract. George was already abroad, serving in the Royal Engineers, but before long Harry returned from South Africa to complete his medical degree at Trinity. Every weekend he brought some of his fellow students home and Mollie teased and amused them, arranging picnics and expeditions to the beaches and hills around Dublin, and parties in the house. On Saturday evening rugs were rolled up in the drawing-room and boys and girls danced to piano music played by one of the sisters. Dublin was still a small city and most of these Trinity families had grown up together and knew one another well.

Mollie enjoyed this social life, where she was a centre of attraction, but she also had to deal at times with bouts of depression and frustration. It seemed then as if she was wasting her precious youth, dissipating it in this provincial suburb of a provincial city, when she longed to explore the Continent, join Nan in London or Paris, and train for the career of her choice. On these occasions, her solace was her violin. She practised it for many hours each day. It released her into a different world where the artistic, creative side of herself could awaken and banish the limitations of daily life.

When she was twenty-one a young man came to the house who began to provide the intellectual stimulation she needed. He was a medical student at Trinity called Bertie Macready, several years junior to Harry but a friend of his and of their cousin George Stack. He was more reserved and thoughtful than most of the boys she knew and Mollie found his silences challenging. He seemed more interested in what was going on in her mind than in her physical charms. He brought books for her to read and discussed with her the Irish literary revival and the work of its poets. He took her to Trinity Library and showed her the *Book of Kells*, the early ninth-century masterpiece created by the monks of St Columba.

'No one knows how long it took to complete,' he told her. 'Probably a whole generation. Look, Mollie, at the decoration of the great capital letters. The designs and symbols are so intricate, yet they all harmonize. They even include pictures of the everyday life of the monks – the birds and animals they saw. What industry, to bring the Gospels to life with such colours, such beauty!' Mollie half closed her eyes and imagined Bertie as one of those monks, devoting his life to his art and his God.

In the National Museum they gazed at the collection of ancient Irish gold objects.

'Those are the bracelets and necklaces the Queens wore,' said Bertie. 'Here is the King's crown. They drank out of these goblets and ate out of these bowls. All beaten gold. Look, they show the old Celtic interlacing designs which are still used today. This was Ireland's heroic age. Yeats has brought it back for us with his poems and plays about Cuchulain and Deirdre.'

And, best of all, they went to the Abbey Theatre to see those plays of Yeats, and others by Synge and Lady Gregory – the three pioneers of the Irish literary movement, which had at last established itself in its own theatre and was receiving acclaim from English as well as Irish critics.

Bertie became Mollie's guide in intellectual and artistic pursuits, but she noticed that he was curiously vulnerable in everyday life. She felt protective when she saw him ill at ease at a party, or disconcerted by a superficial response. Her warmth and responsive companionship became increasingly necessary to him. So, too, did the desire to have her to himself; she was always surrounded by a host of friends.

One evening, when he had brought her some books, and they were alone in the drawing-room at Foxrock, he told her he wanted to share his life with her and asked her to promise herself to him.

His declaration took her by surprise. So did her response, which seemed to come from the realm of her mind and spirit, and to belong to that world of art which Bertie had unfolded for her and which she loved to experience with him. A line of Yeats's came into her mind:

Tread softly, because you tread on my dreams.

This pale young man reminded her of the jester in 'The Cap and Bells':

He bade his heart go to her,
When the owls called out no more;
In a red and quivering garment
It sang to her through the door.

She must try not to hurt him. She asked him to let her think about it.

Mollie thought about little else for the next few weeks. Like most girls of her age, she was in love with the idea of love. Bertie fulfilled her romantic dreams; it was fun to go about with such a good-looking, devoted young man. Marriage occupied a place in the dim far future. She need not worry about that yet. To become engaged would add spice to life and please Bertie; and their companionship, which she valued and enjoyed, could continue.

She rushed to her father with the exciting news.

'He's a fine boy,' her father said. 'Sensitive and intelligent and with a kind of distinction about him. But I wonder if he's strong enough for you, Mollie? You're impulsive, you know, and generous. I'd hate to see you getting engaged just because it's the easiest thing to do. You must be involved body, heart and soul with whomever you marry.'

Mollie told herself that she was. She never doubted her ability to make Bertie happy, and she did not want to part with him. She said yes. There was no official announcement, but her family and friends knew she was promised to Bertie, and she looked radiant enough to justify her decision.

A year or so later Mollie's chance to go abroad came at last. Her fairy-godmother Aunt Molly Geoghegan announced that she and Uncle Willy were going on a six-week tour of the Continent in the spring of 1906 and would like Mollie to accompany them.

The ship for England, the first stage of the journey, left from the little harbour of Kingstown. Standing at the deck-rail Mollie watched the high steeples of its twin churches fade into the distance. The familiar yacht club by the pier, which she had often visited with her father and brothers, merged into the tall colour-washed houses behind it. And beyond, the hills shone with a green she would see only in Ireland. A lone tower on the shore guarded the land. She remembered the day eight years ago when she had waved to perhaps this very steamer, her skirts drenched by the incoming tide, a yearning in her heart.

The ship turned in a wide curve and headed out to sea. Mollie watched the coastline of Ireland disappear. Bertie was still there. She felt a pang of remorse for deserting him. She would miss him. But soon she would be entirely caught up in her new adventure. She hoped that he would understand.

Looking back afterwards on her trip, she remembered most of all a sense of revelation as a new world opened up to her. Aunt Molly and Uncle Willy were leisurely travellers. There was no sense of hurry or strain. Even so, the size of the capital cities at first overwhelmed Mollie. Later, she found that each held its own particular quality – London, its tradition, Paris, its elegance, Rome, its history and its art.

Towards the end of their tour they came back to Paris. Nan

had been there for a year, studying singing. She was no longer a provincial Irish girl; she had become a citizen of Paris. Mollie was most impressed, and copied her, hoping for a similar transformation.

Nan took her to the Louvre where she saw the famous *Winged Victory of Samothrace*, which for many centuries had stood gazing over the clear waters of the Aegean. The strength and beauty of this archaic figure thrilled Mollie. She was to study it in detail later on, when it was to link with her other really memorable experience in Paris – a meeting with a remarkable woman called Mrs Josef Conn.

Nan had come across Mrs Conn in connection with her singing lessons. She was a specialist in remedial health exercises who had developed new theories about physical training for women and was now practising in Paris. Mrs Conn's personality and her ideas struck an immediate chord in Mollie. She talked to her about her health problems, including the rheumatism from which she still suffered, and was told that no woman need be the victim of disease. 'I intend soon to open a training school for students to study my methods,' said Mrs Conn. 'They will discover how to find and keep for themselves a positive health.' Mollie was fascinated. Here might be the outlet and career for which she had long hoped.

At last the wonderful tour came to an end. Nan remained in Paris. Mollie returned to Dublin with her aunt and uncle. It was her birthday. Norah and Charlie had made her a cake with twenty-three candles on it, and an inscription which read: *A jolly birthday to Mary Meta on her safe return from Paris and Many Happy Returns*.

All Mollie's European sophistication evaporated as she hugged them both. Then she unpacked her presents and placed a Parisian hat with a white muslin brim and pink satin ribbons on Norah's schoolgirl head. The next day she poured out her impressions of Europe to Bertie. He listened attentively, but she was aware of a faint barrier rising between them. Bertie was envious. Was he also jealous of experiences he had not been able to share? Mollie's horizons had widened, while his had remained the same. In spite of her fondness for him it was difficult to bridge the gap.

During the next year Mollie thought often of Mrs Conn. Nan reported that a Conn Institute had been established in London. Two-year courses for students were held there, starting each September. To enrol in one would give Mollie the chance to leave home at last and enter the career of her choice. She confided her hopes to Nan, who enthusiastically supported her. Bertie was distressed at the thought of parting with her again, but Theodore and Charlotte approved; and in the summer of 1907 Nan returned to Dublin, took over Mollie's duties to their father, and freed her to go. Mollie entered as a student at the Conn Institute and embarked on a course which was to be the mainspring of her life's work.

Mrs Conn was a pioneer. She had learnt her scientific system of health-building from Sir Frederick McCoy, a distinguished doctor and professor at Melbourne University. His experience as a gynaecologist had led him to believe that the physical poise and balance known to the ancient Greeks should be taught to every prospective mother. Pointing to a picture of the *Discobolus* or the *Winged Victory*, Mrs Conn would show her students examples of 'central control' (the correct training and alignment of the abdominal and pelvic muscles); the lift and expansion of the rib-cage (gained through breathing exercises); and finally the artistic end-product, co-ordination and grace of movement for the whole body.

'The Greeks were free, uncluttered, natural in their response to natural events like the birth of children,' she would declare to the audience at her lecture-demonstrations. 'Throw away your corsets! Move and breathe and live as you were meant to, without restrictions. And do not allow a surgeon to subject you to the knife!'

Her enthusiasm inspired Mollie. Mrs Conn gave remedial tuition to patients sent to her by doctors for conditions such as curvature of the spine, asthma and poor posture. Mollie observed these lessons and realized that she, too, could heal and bring new life to such sufferers.

'You will have to work hard on yourself, Mollie,' Mrs Conn told her. 'Your constitution is not strong. You have already experienced two very serious illnesses. But I can help you. I can bring you to robust health, and then you can pass on your knowledge of how to attain it to others.'

Mollie wrote later about her training:

The more steadily I worked, the more fascinated I became, and the more astonishing the results, probably because the system was so perfectly suited to women. . . . Suddenly, one day, I had an awakening. If this body training was solving for me many of my physical problems, surely in the trained body must lie the solution for many other women as well. . . . The trained body is its 'own best doctor', masseur, pharmacopoeia. . . . It automatically accumulates within itself a power of resistance to disease with each disease resisted, and creates a glorious sense of well-being that colours the whole personality. . . . Thus my health sense was developed, and I was conscious of an inner feeling of freedom and power that has to be experienced to be understood.*

Although Mrs Conn was a visionary, her ideas were in line with the age's new thrust towards women's emancipation. In the dance world, Isadora Duncan was advocating natural movement and freedom from the restrictions of traditional ballet techniques. In the field of education, Madame Osterburg was producing gymnastic teachers who would follow a new career for women, teaching the Swedish Ling system of exercises in girls' schools. In the theatre, Bernard Shaw's heroines were showing an enterprise and independence quite different from the demure Victorian conventions. And on the political front, the suffragettes were gaining ground. Not surprisingly, Mollie developed increasing sympathy for these new attitudes towards women.

She went home to Ireland for holidays, but found it increasingly difficult to convey to Bertie what life in London was like. Dublin seemed small and parochial in comparison, and Bertie himself was becoming tense and strained, working towards his final medical degree and no longer free to be with her on her own terms.

Early in 1909 Mollie decided to share lodgings with her sister Charlie, who was also in London receiving coaching for her final degree in mathematics. They moved into rooms in a hostel in Kensington, where Mollie insisted on practising her Conn

* Mary Bagot Stack, *Building the Body Beautiful*, Chapman and Hall, London, 1931.

exercises for three hours each day in their living-room. She was deeply involved in her course at the Conn Institute and proving herself to be one of Mrs Conn's best pupils. Bertie's letters came regularly, but Mollie, caught up in her new life, could not suppress a sense of dismay when she read them and realized how much he missed her.

The months passed. The sisters worked hard all week. On Sundays they went to church in the morning, and in the evening they attended the Sunday Orchestral Concert at the Royal Albert Hall. Final examinations began to loom for Mollie, in anatomy, physiology, the theory of teaching and public speaking, as well as her practical subjects.

Meanwhile Charlie had become a keen suffragette. She supported the women's cause ardently and hoped to persuade Mollie to do so, too.

One morning she tackled the subject at breakfast. 'Mollie, do come with me to a meeting tonight,' she said. 'Mrs Pankhurst, the suffragette leader, is speaking. She's very impressive. I'm sure you would be interested.'

'I would, Charlie,' Mollie replied, 'but I'm afraid I can't come tonight. I have to go out.'

'Why?'

'Hugh Stack, our cousin, has invited me. He and his sister May came to stay with us in Ireland ages ago. They're coming again this summer holidays. Do you remember them?'

'Indeed I don't.' Charlie was piqued that Mollie seemed to prefer a young man to her suffragette meeting.

'Well, I do. They were very nice. Hugh joined the Indian Army and now he's home on leave. And he's asked me to dine with him tonight.'

Charlie went to her meeting alone. It was crowded and enthusiastic. She felt inspired and walked home from it with new intoxicating phrases ringing through her head: Women must unite and be given the vote! Then they could take more part in politics, selecting who ran the country. Male domination, she reflected, was probably the cause of all the nation's woes.

She was nearing their lodgings when she heard a hansom cab drive up the street behind her. The beat of the horse's hoofs drew nearer. She turned round. There, sitting side by side in the open cab, were Mollie and a young man, presumably Hugh, talking and laughing, totally absorbed in one another. Mollie's cheeks were flushed. Hugh leant attentively towards her. They saw Charlie and both waved to her. Then Hugh took off his hat, put it on the top of his stick and twirled it round and round, smiling at Charlie as though life was the greatest joke. Charlie hurried on homewards, trying not to feel envious.

At breakfast the next day, Mollie's face was radiant. 'I had such a lovely evening with Hugh,' she said.

But Charlie was worried. What about Bertie? Her old fears of her sister's flirtatiousness came back into her mind and would not be dismissed.

A few weeks later Charlie was given a message at the hostel. Miss Stack was wanted in the reception room. She ran downstairs and opened the door. There was Bertie McCready. He looked pale and tired and unhappy, and his height seemed to fill the small room. He seemed at the end of his tether, Charlie thought, unable to bridge the awkwardness between them, and paralysed by a shyness like his own.

'Wrong girl,' she said, hating herself for her flippancy.

She explained that Mollie was out. Bertie was silent. Then he said, 'Just tell her I'm here.'

Mollie was uncommunicative when her sister relayed Bertie's message. She withdrew into herself and went for a long walk alone in the park.

The Albert Memorial loomed impressively above her. Nursemaids passed with their polished prams and well-dressed children. Squirrels stared inquisitively between the bushes, and sparrows hopped over the grass, asking for crumbs. In the flower-beds the spring flowers were being replaced by summer ones. Mollie gazed abstractedly at this scene. It seemed to have no relevance to the hard battle she was fighting within herself.

Bertie had in fact been growing desperate. In letter after letter he told Mollie that he felt she was moving away from him, that they no longer shared the same interests. He had waited for her too long and if he could not now have her full support he would fail his degree. He had even threatened suicide.

'I'm almost there, Mollie,' he wrote. 'Very nearly qualified and able to support you. Marry me now, and I'll succeed. If you don't, I don't know what will happen.'

Mollie did not need to see him to imagine his white face and beseeching eyes. Her old protective feeling for him swept over her. She remembered the precious experiences they had shared, how he had opened her eyes to art and beauty, and given her unquestioning devotion. Her warmth for him revived. It was true that her life had moved into realms where he could not follow; that it might even be taking a new direction whose possibilities dazzled her. But she had promised herself to Bertie. He was depending on her. She was honour-bound to marry him now when he needed her most.

Mollie was impetuous and headstrong. There was no one to advise her. She took no one into her confidence. She made her decision alone. She and Bertie went to a register office, signed their names and were married.

Charlie knew nothing about it at the time. Years later she wrote to Norah:

They never lived together or set up house or anything. She just signed her name and that was all. Nothing more happened. He returned at once to Ireland and she came back to the hostel to me. We were sharing a room and she was always home at nights. I would have known if she had stayed away. She told me nothing. We continued with our work and went on going to the Sunday Orchestral Concerts just as usual.

But Charlie noticed that Mollie was pale and preoccupied and seemed to have lost all her zest for life. She put it down to anxiety about the outcome of her final examinations. Mollie was throwing herself into her training to the exclusion of all else, concentrating all her resources on getting a good diploma. The dark rings under her eyes, thought Charlie, were due to her sitting up so late, studying her anatomy and physiology.

By the end of July the course was over. Mollie passed brilliantly, gaining honours in every subject. Mrs Conn congratulated her as the best pupil and offered her a teaching post on her staff, starting in the autumn.

Pappy will be pleased, thought Mollie. He always wanted us

to be first. But for herself, her success did little to fill the inner void of unease and apprehension which she was experiencing.

'The sooner we get out of London the better,' she said to Charlie. 'I hate these dusty, stuffy streets, the noise, the traffic, the crowds, the heat. . . .'

She found herself longing for Ireland's grey skies, cool winds, soft light and wide stretches of water. Perhaps they would bring her peace.

'Let's go, Charlie,' she said. 'We've done all we can here. Let's go home.'

3

Lover's Leap

Theodore and Charlotte had rented a house for the summer holidays in Portrush, on the northern Antrim coast. It stood on a headland above the sea, its front windows looking westwards to the hills of Inishowen far away on the Donegal horizon. A garden surrounded it, full of wind-blown flowers, and beyond was short-cropped turf, a thin layer on the cliffs which fell sheer to the rocks and waves below. A half-circle of sandy beach stretched out to the harbour and its fishing-boats. There a lighthouse gleamed by day and flashed in the dark by night, and in storms the groan of a bell-buoy sounded its note of warning.

Mollie and Charlie came there straight from London, catching a boat across the Irish Channel, and then a train to Portrush. On the journey Mollie's thoughts were dominated by her cousin, Hugh.

On their evening out together they had compared family notes – they shared a great-grandfather – and Hugh told her he had been born in India. Both his father and his grandfather had served there; his father Edward Stack in the Indian Civil Service, and his grandfather George Bagot Stack in the East India Company, which he had joined in 1838, later serving on General Napier's staff in Sind. Both these men had died young – his grandfather at thirty-four, his father at thirty-seven.

Hugh was less than two when his father died. His mother Rosalie moved to England, and in 1891 she married Henry Luttman-Johnson, a colleague and friend of Hugh's father in the Indian Civil Service. This man became a second father to

Hugh and his sister May, and when he retired they were brought up at his homes in London and Sussex, together with their two half-brothers Freddy and Billy Luttman-Johnson, twins born in 1892.

Henry and Rosalie told Hugh much about India, and his upbringing was rich in Indian associations. From a young age he longed to return there. He had gone to Winchester College, which was Henry's old school, and to Sandhurst, where he gained his commission in the Indian Army in 1905. He then travelled straight to India, joining first the 60th King's Royal Rifles, and after a year his permanent regiment, the 2nd Battalion, 8th Gurkha Rifles. This was his first home leave.

When they met in London Hugh's attraction to Mollie was immediate. He had tried to see her again, but she had evaded a meeting, sensing how dangerous it could be. Now he and his sister May were coming to stay with her family and would be in Ireland in a few days' time.

Mollie was in a terrible situation. She had told no one but Nan of her marriage to Bertie and now found it impossible to confide in any other member of her family, even her father. Lying awake in bed that night, listening to the eerie groan of the bell-buoy, restless thoughts milled round endlessly in her head.

'I *will* be sensible,' she said to herself. 'I *will* keep Hugh at arm's length. I *will* remember that I must.'

But at the sight of Hugh a few days later, all her good resolutions foundered. He came striding down the path to the house, took her hand, and said, 'Oh, Mollie, I *am* so glad to see you again.'

His greeting was so spontaneous and heartfelt that she laughed.

'Where have you been hiding all this time?' he continued. 'You were so elusive. But I've run you to earth at last.' He beamed at her triumphantly, then turned to greet the other members of the family.

Hugh was twenty-four at the time of this Irish visit. He had spent four years in India and his life there had given him powers of decision and command. He looked strong and soldierly, Mollie thought, yet sensitive in his attention to her parents, and able to joke with Charlie and Norah, teasing them like an elder brother. When he laughed, his brown eyes crinkled up at the corners. And he laughed a lot.

'You're very welcome here, both of you,' said her father, as her mother greeted and kissed them.

The family arranged expeditions for their guests, including one to the Giant's Causeway, a famous geological curiosity which lay a few miles away along the coast.

It was an astonishing place. Row upon row of basalt columns, most of them hexagonal in shape and some up to forty feet in height, were thrown together, creating a lunar landscape that spread over a wide area and ended in a gaunt sea wall. Through this scene of desolation ran the Causeway, the tops of its columns packed tightly together to form stepping-stones that stretched from the foot of the cliff to the sea.

They walked down it and then along a narrow path past amphitheatres with mythical names – the Honeycomb, the Wishing Chair, the King and his Nobles, and Lover's Leap – until they climbed a wooden staircase to the crest of Benbane Head. The way back lay along the top of the cliff.

'But first, a rest,' said Mollie. 'I'm exhausted.' She dropped on to the grass with Hugh beside her, while the others strolled ahead.

A fresh salt wind blew in from the sea and piles of cumulus cloud moved slowly across the sky. They sat on the cliff-top, Mollie playing with the ribbons of her hat which lay on the grass beside her. Hugh began to talk and she listened, totally absorbed, as he described his Gurkha soldiers, the hill-station of his regiment, the Himalayas. . . .

'They're so beautiful, those mountains, Mollie. Unbeliev-able. Somehow untouched, unsullied. I wish you'd come to India one day and see them.'

'Oh, Hugh, if only I could!' Her face darkened and she bent her head.

'Why couldn't you?'

'Well, I couldn't afford it, for one thing. But apart from that I have things I must do here.'

'What things?'

Mollie frowned. 'Don't press me, Hugh,' she said. 'I can't tell you.'

She rose abruptly to her feet, and at that moment a gust of wind blew along the headland, lifted her hat from the ground and sent it sailing over the cliff. They both ran to the edge and watched it descend, floating like a bird, until it reached a ledge a third of the way down, where it settled on a jutting stone.

'My lovely sailor hat!' wailed Mollie.

'I'll get it for you,' said Hugh.

'No, Hugh, don't . . . *don't*. . . .' But her warning came too late. Hugh had already turned to face the cliff and was letting himself down inch by inch, feeling for minute footholds and transferring his weight carefully from hand to hand. Far below lay a mass of jagged rocks and pebbles.

Mollie watched, terrified. She was appalled by the danger – too appalled to realize what an expert climber he was.

He reached the ledge, stood on it, took a good hold with one hand and with the other lifted the hat from its perch and clapped it on his head. Then he looked up, grinning, and said, 'I'm coming back.'

Mollie held her breath and clenched her palms until the nails dug into her flesh. She saw his hands reach over the cliff-top, inch along it, find a crack and a stout piece of grass, pull, and he was up, breathing hard, his face red with the effort and her hat still perched on his head. She laughed, half-crying with relief; then, without thinking, she flung her arms round his neck and kissed him on the cheek.

'Oh, Hugh, I was so frightened for you,' she said. He held her waist with one hand and with the other set her hat back on her head. She felt him trembling, not only with the effort of the climb. He tied the ribbons under her chin. Then he leant forward and kissed her.

'Now I've found you again,' he said, 'I'm not going to let you go, Mollie. Not ever.'

There was a sheltered corner of the garden at Portrush where Theodore sat most mornings. He was protected from the wind by a wing of the house and a hedge, but had an open view of the sea. In his wheelchair, a rug over his knees, he could read undisturbed, every now and then lifting his eyes to the foam-flecked waves. Hugh found him in this place a few days after their expedition to the Giant's Causeway. He drew up a chair, while Theodore put down his book and prepared to talk, lifting his ear-trumpet to his ear and leaning forward with an expression of concentration on his face.

'Well, Hugh,' he said, 'how are you enjoying being an Irishman in Ireland?'

'Very much,' said Hugh. 'All sorts of deep race memories are assailing me! But there are some things I don't understand.'

'Such as?'

'Your politics. Why should you be proud of being in the British Empire and yet wish for Home Rule?'

Theodore summoned up his powers of exposition.

'The country is very deeply divided,' he said. 'The North – Ulster – as a whole is against Home Rule. They think it would be a betrayal of their British heritage and disloyal to the Crown. On the other hand, the extreme Catholic faction in the South – the Sinn Fein – think Home Rule doesn't go nearly far enough. They want total independence from England. Between these two are the main majority of the people who would like Ireland to govern itself, but still remain part of the empire.'

'Well, that sounds sensible enough,' said Hugh. 'Why can't it be achieved?'

'The Liberal Party in England has been trying to achieve it ever since Gladstone brought in the first Home Rule Bill in 1886. I remember the hopes that aroused. But it was defeated, and so was its successor in 1892. There were so many forces against it – the Conservatives, the House of Lords, the Ulster Unionists. All these still exist, but in spite of that I hope the Liberals will launch a third Home Rule Bill.'

He paused, and gathered his strength to continue.

'You'd support it?' said Hugh.

'I would. It seems to me the one hope for Ireland. The only basis for unity. Without it, violence will get the upper hand. We're a violent people, Hugh. We feel strongly.'

Hugh nodded, then asked abruptly, 'If there was another war, would Ireland fight side by side with England?'

Theodore stared at him, amazed, even adjusted his ear-trumpet to make sure he had heard right.

'Of course,' he said. 'Without any doubt. We'd never let England fight alone. Anyway, Irishmen love a battle.'

Hugh laughed, then grew serious again. 'I think there's a real possibility another war may come,' he said. 'My stepfather was talking about it in London. It would be the end of the world as we know it. It makes one want to live life to the full – now.'

Theodore's face softened as he gazed at the sea before bringing his eyes back to Hugh.

'I've always told Mollie,' he said, 'be thankful for every day and live it as though it was your last. I try to do that even now.'

He sank back in his chair, tired with the effort of talking. Hugh made to leave, but Theodore held out a detaining hand. He seemed to be reflecting. Then he said, 'I've been thinking about Mollie. And you. I'm an old man now but I remember what it was like to be young and in love. And to have difficulties in the way.' He paused, then continued, 'Mollie hasn't confided in me, but I know she's having a hard time. A conflict of heart and head. She'll tell you, Hugh. You're involved in it. And you can help her. Please do.'

His voice died away and he bowed his head. Hugh stood up. He laid his hand on Theodore's bent shoulder and felt the old man respond. Then he turned to go, while Theodore sat on alone, listening to the cry of the gulls as they wheeled above the sea.

For the last night of May's and Hugh's visit – the night of the full moon – a plan had been made to take a picnic supper to Dunluce Castle. But on the morning of the expedition May woke with a sick headache and had to remain in bed. Norah volunteered to stay with her and Charlie, as usual, had work to do. So finally only Mollie and Hugh set off, driving in an Irish jaunting-car through the long summer twilight, talking little, serious and preoccupied.

The castle stood on a precipitous headland. Its gaunt grey ruins, weathered by time, seemed as much part of the landscape as the cliff-face on which they were poised. High walls and towers threw dark shadows across the grass and the scent of thyme was mixed with the smell of the sea. Mollie and Hugh climbed the steep slope to the ruins in silence, he carrying the picnic basket, she swinging her hat by its ribbons. They reached the top.

'An old Irish fort used to stand here,' said Mollie. 'The early Christians and Vikings came too. One can feel the past very strongly here, as one can everywhere in Ireland.'

Hugh put down the basket, and Mollie gathered a small posy of the blue flower of Dunluce, clustering at the foot of the walls, and placed it in his buttonhole.

'Where would you like to have our picnic?' she asked.

'Let's go to the farthest point, right out over the sea,' Hugh replied.

So they ate their supper on the cliff-top high above the Atlantic and heard the waves pounding against the rocks two hundred feet below. The suck and surge and slap of the water reverberated through the air and the fall of spray was as sharp as shrapnel. Further out, the darkening mass heaved and billowed. A wide silver path began to stretch across it, leading to the horizon and the slowly rising moon.

The beauty was dazzling but daunting also. Involuntarily they drew closer together, Mollie's face a white oval in the gathering dusk. Hugh turned to it.

'You've told me that one can feel the past very strongly in Ireland,' he said. 'But I want to talk to you about the future.'

The moon rose and climbed up the dark sky. A few stars appeared, paled by its light. Its reflection on the sea became more and more brilliant, points of water dancing in it as though alive. The waves' surge continued. And through it all Hugh and Mollie sat, talking and talking. They were so still, so absorbed in one another, that a small night animal which drew near remained and stared at them, unfrightened.

When at last they rose to their feet and, arm in arm, started the descent, no secrets remained between them. The moon had risen high in the sky, banishing shadows from their path. And Mollie's mind and heart were as clear and luminous as its light.

Mollie wrote to Nan, who had spent August in London and who, alone of the family, knew about her marriage to Bertie. She described Hugh's arrival in Portrush, their growing attachment, her efforts to resist it, her failure, and finally the realization that they loved each other and always would.

I'd never dreamt I could be so happy. Of course, I shall have
to get a divorce. Bertie will agree, won't he? He must. I've
told Mother. She was shocked, but then wonderfully helpful
and we're both coming over to London very soon to see about
the divorce. . . .

Nan folded the letter carefully and put it back in the
envelope. Typical Mollie, she thought. Completely caught up
with her present feelings, casting all difficulties aside. I don't
suppose for one moment that Bertie will agree. Why should he?
And what about Hugh's family? They'll almost certainly
object.

But when Mollie and her mother arrived a few days later,
Nan's fears for her took second place to the aura which now
surrounded her sister. There was something about her Nan had
never seen before – the mysterious look of a girl deeply in love.

'I'm *sure* – sure at last,' she said to Nan. 'Nothing will ever
alter the way I feel.'

'And does Hugh feel the same?'

'Yes.' There was a silence between them as Nan adjusted
herself to this new Mollie. Then she continued, 'Of course I
know the world won't see it the way we do. There'll be all sorts
of obstacles and objections. But they don't really matter. Even
if I never saw Hugh again what I have now couldn't be taken
away from me.'

'Have you told Bertie?'

'Yes. I wrote to him. I'm waiting for a reply.'

Nan got up and put her arms round her sister. Mollie's
happiness was so overwhelming, yet in Nan's mind so
precarious, that she wanted to be physically close to her.
'Whatever happens, I'll help you,' she said.

Mollie took up her new post on Mrs Conn's staff and found its
professional requirements a relief after the turbulent emotions
she had been experiencing. She was now helping to train Mrs
Conn's students and assisting with her private patients, putting
the theory she had learnt into practice and discovering new
ways of interesting her pupils each day.

The work was demanding. Her status as a tutor needed

commitment, as well as a sympathetic ear for her students' queries. In giving what she hoped was wise advice she often thought, If only they knew what a crisis my own life is in! Personal problems could be put aside during working hours, but outside they were multiplying.

Bertie had written to say he could not bear the idea of a divorce. 'I've waited so long for you, Mollie,' he said. 'How can you suggest our parting when we're only just married? I love you and I trusted you. I can't give you up.'

Then early in October May came to see her. She brought a note from Hugh. Mollie tore it open, eagerly read its contents and then looked up, her face transformed. 'He wants to meet me tomorrow.'

'I know,' said May. 'But first of all, will you let me talk to you?'

May told Mollie that she knew Hugh loved her and was determined to marry her at any cost, but that if he did so there would be a complete rift with his family.

'My mother can't possibly approve of a divorced woman marrying her son,' she warned.

'Do you know the circumstances of my marriage?' Mollie asked.

'I do,' May answered gently. 'I'm not blaming you. I'm only telling you what the world will say. You will be labelled as a divorced woman, whatever the rights and wrongs of the case. Then there's the question of Hugh's career. Indian Army officers are not encouraged – often not allowed – to marry until they are captains. In Hugh's case, that won't be for five more years. I don't think his colonel would give him leave to marry sooner, even if all the circumstances were favourable. As it is . . . '

May's voice trailed away, overcome by the stricken look on Mollie's face.

'Has Hugh asked you to say all this to me?'

'Of course not. He thinks very differently. It's just because of his obstinacy that I felt I had to talk to you before you see him again.'

Mollie spent a sleepless night. May's words hammered round and round in her mind. By midnight she had decided she must give up Hugh, whatever he said. Voices came to her out of

the darkness: '*His career*', '*shame and dishonour*', '*divorced woman*'.
By dawn she had reversed the decision. New voices sounded:
'*You were made for each other.*' '*Don't throw away love.*' '*Believe in
yourselves.*' The night seemed endless. At last morning came.
She dressed for work with hardly the strength or the will to put
on something pretty for later on.

They met at the Cavalry Club. Mollie arrived breathless. She
had half run down Piccadilly, her cheeks flaming and her hair
unruly, in case she should be late. Hugh was waiting on the
doorstep. He took her inside and guided her to a sofa in a quiet
alcove where they could be alone. And there, amid the chintz
covers and sporting prints, the silver trophies and small
mahogany tables, they talked of their future.

An old waiter brought them tea and buttered toast under a
silver cover. It remained untouched.

Hugh listened while Mollie expressed her fears for him, her
doubts, her efforts at renunciation. He took each statement
seriously, minimizing nothing. Then he said, 'I've told you,
Mollie. Now that I've found you I'm never going to let you go.
We must trust each other completely. That's all that really
matters.' He leant forward and took her hands. 'Everything
will come right in the end,' he insisted, 'even though we may
have to wait for some time. Will you mind?'

'Mind? I'd wait for ever.'

'Mollie, darling, don't look so tragic!'

'Your family?'

'I'll tell them later, when we know exactly what has to be
done. May loves you already. My mother will, as soon as she
knows you. Have faith, Mollie.'

He felt in his pocket, then pressed a small package into her
hand and closed her fingers round it. 'Keep this till later.'

He dropped her home in a hansom cab, as on their first
evening out together. She watched him drive away, both of
them waving until he was out of sight, half of herself going with
him. His leave was almost at an end. She would not see him
again.

Indoors, Nan was waiting.

'Look what Hugh gave me,' said Mollie.

She drew the little package from her bag and opened it. On a card was pinned a silver brooch made of two crossed kukries with a figure eight above them. It was Hugh's regimental badge. Below, in his handwriting, were the words of the Gurkha motto: *I will keep faith.*

During that autumn Theodore and Charlie were alone in the house in Foxrock. Neither had been told of Mollie's marriage and impending divorce – Theodore because of his precarious health, Charlie because it would upset her pattern of work. Charlie could see that her father had grown very frail. The holiday in Portrush had not restored him, as she hoped it would. This was the first time her mother had ever left him since his illness began. Why didn't she and Mollie – his favourite daughter – come back? He needed them both.

Charlie dreaded the return of Theodore's attacks. And in early December it happened. The attack lasted for about twenty minutes and then suddenly Theodore died. His weak heart had finally succumbed. Charlie sat on beside her father, silent and dry-eyed, holding his hand until the doctor came and closed his eyes. He was sixty-one years old.

The family assembled in Dublin. Mollie felt heart-broken at her father's loss and guilty that her mother had not been at his side. In clearing up his legal affairs with their Dublin solicitor she took the opportunity to consult him about her divorce. She had hoped, and been almost sure, it would be easy to procure, because her marriage had never been consummated. But the solicitor told her firmly that the only way to get a divorce was for evidence of adultery to be produced.

'This is usually arranged by the husband,' he explained. 'Even if the wife is the guilty party, the man generally takes the blame.'

'But I can't ask Bertie to do that,' said Mollie to Nan as they lay that evening on their beds in the room they still shared at Foxrock. 'Even if he agreed it would be untrue, and anyway a dreadful affront to him. I am the guilty one. I must take the blame myself.'

'You'll have to write to Hugh,' Nan replied. 'You'll have to write to him and explain. He'll have to get leave and come back and produce the evidence with you.'

Mollie's eyes widened in horror. '*Nan!* It would be the end of his army career.'

'You must risk that. Look, Mollie, you're always saying you believe in the truth and want to live by the truth. Now's the time to prove it. I'm sure Hugh will agree and help you, if you give him a chance.'

Hugh asked his colonel for compassionate leave to return home on urgent family business, and in February 1910 he and Mollie met at an hotel in London.

He registered at the desk, signed his name in the book, and then, suddenly, there was Mollie beside him, alive, beautiful, the colour coming and going in her cheeks.

Hugh turned and saw her standing there with beseeching eyes, her face a mixture of shyness, amusement and embarrassment.

'Oh, Hugh, you've come,' she said. 'We've got separate rooms, but they had to have a connecting door!'

Hugh burst into laughter. 'Mollie, darling,' he cried. He hugged her, then slipped his arm through hers and led her away.

> He who bends to himself a Joy
> Doth the winged life destroy.
> But he who kisses the Joy as it flies
> Lives in Eternity's sunrise.

Mollie thought often of Blake's poem in the crowded days that followed. Hugh's short leave was flying past. Together they had found the 'winged life', felt its touch. But soon they must let it go. Hugh talked to her of the yogic wisdom he had learnt in India. How beyond the world of appearances was the world of reality, unchanging, undiminished, 'Eternity's sunrise'.

'In loving each other, we've had a glimpse of it,' he said. 'But we can't possess it. Not now, perhaps not ever. All we can do is to wait and trust in our destiny.'

He seemed to have grown up overnight, Mollie thought, to have reached a maturity and strength she had always divined but not seen before.

'I've told my mother,' he continued. 'I couldn't go on living a lie with her. She was very upset. I think she hopes the divorce won't go through. But she knows I won't change.'

His last evening came and they spent it together, spinning out the hours until the early morning. As they said goodbye, he told her, 'I'll be with you all the time. Never forget that.' Then he walked home under the winter stars.

How far away they seem! he thought. In India you can pluck them out of the sky. Will Mollie ever see them in India?

After Hugh's departure, Mollie consulted another solicitor in London. He advised her to send the evidence of adultery with an accompanying letter to her husband, in the hope that he might now agree to a divorce. Mollie carried out these instructions and waited. At last a letter came from a Dublin solicitor, acting on Bertie's behalf. It informed her that a petition for divorce had been filed by her husband, and the case should come before the courts in the next few months. Her evidence would be used and made public in court, but it was not necessary for her to attend the hearing.

Mollie prepared herself for the ordeal which lay ahead.

'Do you think it can be kept quiet?' she asked Nan, 'or will everyone know?'

'I think it's a matter of luck,' Nan replied. 'I suppose it just depends on whether a reporter is at the court on that day or not.'

The months passed. At last Mollie was given the date when her case would be heard. Soon after, two letters arrived for her in London as she and Nan sat at breakfast. The first was from her Dublin solicitor. Her case had come before the court and the judge had granted a decree nisi to Bertie. She must allow six months or so for the decree to be made absolute. Then, if nothing happened to alter the judge's decision, she would be free.

Mollie tossed the piece of paper across the table to Nan and opened the second letter. It was from Charlie. It enclosed a press cutting – the front page of the *Irish Times*. There, for all the world to see, was her letter to Bertie, pleading for a divorce, along with the evidence she had provided of adultery.

'Oh, Mollie, why did you do it?' wrote Charlie. 'Why didn't you tell me? I knew nothing about it. The shock. The shame and the scandal. How will we live through them? It's awful for you but it's awful for your family too. And for Hugh and his family. And for Bertie. So many people will be hurt by your action. I can only thank God that Pappy is no longer alive. He, at any rate, will be spared this.'

Mollie stared unbelievingly at the letter and the cutting, trembling in her hand. Then the strain of the last few months overwhelmed her. She pushed away her cup and plate, laid her head on her folded arms, and sobbed and sobbed, her tears making a widening damp patch on the breakfast table.

In his hill-station beside the Himalayas, Hugh stood in his colonel's office. He fixed his eyes on a large relief map on the wall behind the desk, while the colonel read the press cutting from the *Irish Times* which Hugh had laid before him. There was a long silence. Then the colonel cleared his throat and raised his head.

'Well, Hugh,' he said, 'you can't possibly expect me to approve of this.' He flipped the cutting away to a corner of his desk and stared at Hugh with cold blue eyes. Hugh returned his gaze.

'I don't, sir.'

'Did you know that this would be the outcome of your leave?'

'Yes, sir. But not that it would receive so much publicity.'

'That's beside the point. It's unfortunate, of course. But what matters is that I gave you compassionate leave and you used it to do something which would discredit the regiment.'

'Yes, sir.' Hugh transferred his eyes from the colonel's to the map and waited.

'Why did you do it?'

'I felt I had to, sir. There was no choice. It seemed the honourable and straightforward thing to do.'

'Even if it meant the end of your career in the Indian Army?'

'I had to risk that, sir.'

'Do you hope to marry this Mrs Macready?'

Hugh flinched at the sound of the alien name. 'I do, sir.'

'Tell me about her.'

Hugh looked in doubt at the colonel, whose eyes had not softened, then told him briefly the circumstances of Mollie's marriage. There was another long silence.

At last the colonel said, 'I can't minimize the seriousness of what you've done. I don't doubt your word or your motives, but men have been relieved of their commissions for less. As for marriage – that must wait. You will have to prove to me afresh your commitment to the regiment. You will also have to gain more seniority before we can even consider it. This', he took up the cutting with an expression of distaste, 'need go no further. The fewer people that see it, the better.'

Deliberately he folded the piece of newspaper twice, tore it into four pieces and dropped them into an elephant-hoof waste-paper basket. He gave Hugh one more icy stare, then said, 'That is all. As far as I am concerned the matter is at an end.'

'Thank you, sir.' Hugh turned smartly on his heel and left the room.

Mollie received an account of Hugh's interview as she was packing up to leave London. 'Poor Hugh!' she said aloud. But his letter reassured her greatly. It ended with a quotation from the poet Blake: 'The soul of sweet delight can never be defiled.'

We must remember that, thought Mollie.

The Conn Institute had asked her to go to Manchester, to start classes there and carry its work to the North of England. After a year on Mrs Conn's staff she was well qualified to do this; and with her own practice she would be able to make enough money to pay off the debt she had contracted for her training fees. Her mother offered to come with her and rent a house which could be their home. So in the autumn of 1910 they both set off.

The suburb of Altrincham, where they were to live, contained prosperous middle-class homes where potential pupils for Mollie might well reside, alongside poor working-class districts that reminded her of the slums of Dublin. She soon realized that in the industrial North life was more polarized than in the South. There were extremes of wealth and poverty: industrial barons who lived in great luxury with an ostentatious display of their possessions; and workers who produced the marketable goods that brought prosperity, but who were experiencing a continued drop in their real wages, as prices and the cost of living rose.

Throughout 1910 a new mood of unrest was developing. The labour force increasingly turned to the trade unions to defend their interests and the weapon of the strike was used more frequently against employers. Sometimes the confrontations became violent, as relations deteriorated between the industrialists and their work-forces.

Mollie resolved that her work in Manchester must be not only for the privileged few. She would get herself established, then try to extend it to the areas where it was most needed; where poverty and malnutrition brought disease and where knowledge of hygiene and positive health were absent.

The first step was a lecture-demonstration. Mollie called on doctors to whom she had introductions, gave interviews to the press, had leaflets displayed in libraries and shops, and gave talks to groups of women in clubs. She hired a hall which held a hundred people, arranged for a demonstrator who would show the exercises and ordered a jade-green velvet dress which she hoped would increase her presence on the platform. Her mother and Norah, who had travelled from Ireland specially, decorated the hall and ushered in the audience. And by three o'clock, when the lecture was to begin, every seat was full.

Mollie walked on to the stage in her jade-green dress and immediately felt a wave of sympathy and interest from the audience.

What she was advocating was something new – that women should take themselves in hand, learn to prevent the ailments that ignorance fostered, and rely not only on medical cures but also on their own powers of positive health and strength, built up through the right form of exercise. She soon began to inspire her audience – and she amused them, too, with comic illustrations of the wrong and right way to sit, stand and walk. Her assistant (clad in a white satin blouse and long black satin knickers, the daring uniform of the Conn Institute) demonstrated exercises for each part of the body with suppleness, confidence and grace. And between them they convinced the women in the audience that they too could learn this technique and would benefit by it.

The lecture was followed by tea. Mollie came down off the platform and talked to people individually. At close range, she looked an even better advertisement for her system, with her heightened colour, expressive eyes and unbounded enthusiasm. People were attracted and impressed. In the course of half an hour Norah had booked fifty appointments.

Very soon Mollie's days were filled with individual patients sent to her by doctors and small classes of women anxious to improve their health and physique. She soon established a close relationship with her pupils. She was now teaching the general public rather than specialized students, and she realized that the hard individual effort required must be tempered with a sense of enjoyment and fun. Humour and sympathy came easily to her, but these had to be mixed with firmness to gain results, and results she was determined to achieve. Her practice grew and she made many friends.

One of these was the wife of a mill-owner who employed large numbers of girls and women. She had already organized welfare work for them and knew the difficult circumstances in which most of them lived. She told Mollie about them and Mollie saw her opportunity.

'Let's experiment with a class twice a week,' she told her friend. 'If you can gather them together, I'll give them a talk and we'll see what response we get.'

This lecture-demonstration was very different from the opening one in Manchester, several weeks before. The women were packed into a small room. They sat on chairs in their working clothes, signs of tiredness and strain on their faces. They were shy and self-conscious, suspicious of being patronized. And most of them were eager to go home.

Mollie, too, wore her working clothes. She spoke to them directly and urgently, getting in touch with their fears as well as their hopes, and feeling the emanations of exhaustion and doubt that came from this audience. She showed them some of the exercises, explaining what each one was for, made them laugh at and with her, told them of individual cases she had been able to help. And finally she said, 'Now let's try all this out. Push away your chairs, and we'll have a short class here and now.'

Crowded, breathless, laughing and sweating, they went through a few of her exercises, and by the end of half an hour Mollie had gained a number of new disciples. She wondered if any would come back next week. In fact, when they assembled again the class had swollen to twice its number and had to be moved into a larger room.

This work continued for the rest of Mollie's stay in Manchester. She met the mill-girls twice a week after working hours, and in addition visited those who needed individual treatment in their homes. She wrote to Norah:

> They all lead frightful lives. I wish I could do more to help them. Often, when I visit them, I find the man of the family is out of work or on strike or drunk. And yet they have such courage and humour. You'd be amazed how much we laugh in the classes. I make them wash their faces before they come, and they promise me they'll wash again when they go home. . . . The division between them and my prosperous paying pupils is immense and so unfair, it seems to me.

As well as the mill classes, Mollie offered to teach her exercises to the Girl Guides, a movement she much admired. She also held classes for poor children on Saturday afternoons, and at Christmas time arranged a party for them. Within a year she had built up a rewarding structure of work in Manchester.

Early in 1911 her divorce was made absolute. She wrote this news to Hugh, who had just returned from a month-long Gurkha recruiting trip in the mountains of Nepal. They were now free to marry. But Hugh's mother had asked them to wait for another year.

'I feel I ought to say "yes",' Hugh wrote. 'You and I know we won't change, but we have to convince her and others. It's doubtful anyway if I could get permission from my Colonel just yet.'

Mollie agreed. So the year of 1911 passed with them still separated, while in Europe fateful preparations were being made for the tragedy which would soon engulf the world.

4

The Far Snows

Mollie and Hugh were married in London on 10 March 1912 at the City Temple, a United Reformed church she had attended during her London years. The Reverend R.J. Campbell, its famous preacher and minister, performed the ceremony. All Mollie's family were there, although Hugh's were not. His mother had been unable to reconcile herself to her son's marriage to a divorced woman in a Free Church.

Spring sunshine streamed through the plain glass windows and daffodils lightened the austerity of the church. Always afterwards their fresh faint scent reminded Mollie of that day. Her long separation from Hugh was over at last.

On her honeymoon in Devon she wrote to Norah: 'If you can imagine to yourself the most supreme happiness and then double and treble it, you will have a faint idea of what I am feeling now. Hugh is absolutely perfect and there's nothing we don't understand about each other.'

During this time Hugh told Mollie about Lansdowne, the permanent hill-station where they would live, to prepare her for the move to India. A battalion of Hugh's regiment – the 2nd Battalion, 8th Gurkha Rifles – occupied Lansdowne, together with the Garhwal Rifles whose men were recruited from the district around.

'It's a military station,' said Hugh. 'A bugle plays reveille and wakes you in the morning, and the last post puts you to sleep at night. The regiment is like a family – a group of people closely involved with one another. And I'm afraid it's a male-oriented society. Wives acquire the rank of their

63

husbands!'

For the first year of his military service in India, Hugh had been posted to a British regiment – the 60th King's Royal Rifles. This happened to all young subalterns. They had to learn the ropes: how to adjust to India, how to manage men, how to put the theory they had learnt at Sandhurst into practice.

'We went on manoeuvres to Rawalpindi, a hill-station near the north-west frontier, and there I saw Gurkhas for the first time,' said Hugh. 'I was most impressed with their smartness and discipline.'

Later, when he joined them at Lansdowne, Hugh realized that the grins on their brown Mongolian faces masked a keen observation of their officers' foibles and shortcomings.

'They're wonderful mimics,' he told Mollie. 'When you visit a Gurkha officers' or NCOs' mess it usually ends in gales of laughter. They're tremendously loyal but also fiercely independent. Each of them is his own man.'

Hugh had now been a lieutenant in the 2nd Battalion, 8th Gurkhas for three years. He explained that up to then he had been living in subalterns' quarters, which consisted of a bedroom with a washroom attached, containing only a zinc tub and an enamel wash-basin. A hole in the wall let the water out and the snakes in. When you wanted a bath you shouted for the *mehter*, or sweeper, who was sitting nearby all day, and water and towels appeared in due course.

'But you won't have to experience anything like that, Mollie,' he reassured her. 'We'll have a bungalow of our own, and our own servants. How I'm longing to show it to you!'

They had only a few days in Devon, and spent the last week of Hugh's leave in Ireland. Norah saw them off from Kingstown on the steamer that Mollie had watched sail away into the open sea so long ago. Together she and Hugh leant over the deck-rail to wave goodbye and Norah thought she had never seen two people look more radiantly happy.

They travelled overland to Marseilles, sailed to Bombay, landed in intense heat, crawled across the burning plains in a train which took several days and finally reached the railhead.

Their gear was transferred into ox-carts and they rode ahead, up a mountain path into the foothills of the Himalayas.

Trees covered the lower slopes, and the path wove in and out of their shade. Its surface was rough, gutted with the deep tracks of carts. It turned as it ascended, bringing into view first the valley below with its broad stony river and then clusters of houses above, clinging precariously to the steep hillside.

Glades opened in the woods on either side of the track, crossed by beams of sunlight and camouflaged by the play of light and shade. At the end of one of them a huge elephant grazed. Langur monkeys leapt among the trees and ran beside the path, keeping pace with Hugh and Mollie and gazing at them with mournful eyes. The horses climbed slowly. Except for the creak of their saddles and the soft pad of their hoofs there was no noise.

Mollie rode in a kind of trance, mesmerized by the regular motion of her horse, the silence of the forest and the strangeness of the scene. Every now and then Hugh turned round in his saddle to smile at her, but he did not speak. He seemed to know that whatever discomfort she might feel from the heat, the flies and the ache of muscles unused to riding, nothing must be allowed to break the spell of this journey.

The path climbed more steeply. Now they were out in the open above the trees, heading towards a small village with terraced fields of bright mustard, and winding drystone walls. A group of young children stood by the wayside. Hugh called a greeting to them and they hid their faces and dispersed like a flock of startled birds. The smell of wood-smoke mingled with that of pine.

Beyond the village the path narrowed. It skirted round terraced slopes, led in and out of clusters of wooden houses and made detours to avoid landslides which had devastated some sections of the hill. The skyline above drew nearer. Mollie could see its serrated trees distinctly, and her eyes swept over the slopes below, falling in ledges, gorges and forests to the valley, now far away and in shadow.

The horses climbed to the crest. Lansdowne, Hugh's hill-station, with its bungalows, cantonment, parade-ground and bazaar, appeared before them. A bugle sounded on the still air. The sun grew in size as it sank in the deepening sky. Hugh

turned to Mollie, his face lit by the glow. He brought his horse
to stand beside hers, and leant over to place a hand on her
bridle. They gazed in silence at the overpowering white frieze
on the horizon. At last, together, they were within sight of the
Himalayas.

Their home stood in its own grounds in the married quarters. It
was a spacious bungalow with a veranda, a lawn and a view of
the distant snow. The servants were lined up outside the house
to greet them, each dressed in immaculate white with a red
band round his turban and a red cummerbund round his waist.
Hugh introduced them one by one – the *khitmagar* who was head
of the household, the cook, the groom, and the gardener.

'They each have several assistants,' Hugh said. 'You'll see,
there's a sort of feudal relationship with the servants. We feel
responsible when they're ill or have family troubles. It's a kind
of belonging – we to them, and they to us.'

After dinner they sat in two wicker chairs on the veranda
watching the moon rise in the clear mountain air.

'I feel completely at home already,' said Mollie.

'I'm so happy you're here. I don't want to share you with
anybody,' Hugh answered. 'But I'll have to. You must pay
some calls, and we must ask the CO to dinner.'

'Let me find my feet with the servants first. They seem to be
prepared to do everything. The *ayah* would have bathed me and
dressed me if I'd let her.'

Hugh laughed. 'That's typical. You'll find the *khitmagar* will
look after the household completely for you. The less you
interfere the better. He'll allow you to arrange the flowers and
order the meals.'

'Kind of him! And the other wives?'

'You'll meet them all in due course. They get together at the
moorghi-kana, the hen-house as it's called, at the Club.'

'That's where all the gossip and scandal starts?'

'I suppose so.'

'Will they approve of me?' Mollie looked anxiously at Hugh.
He got up from his chair and moved to stand behind her,
slipping his hands over her shoulders and pressing them
reassuringly. Together they gazed at the brilliant night sky.

'Just be yourself, Mollie, darling,' he said. 'Your radiant, beautiful self. No one could fail to love you.'

Hugh's colonel and his wife and some other senior officers and their wives came to dinner. Mollie had taken immense pains over the occasion, informing the cook that it was a *burra khana*, a big dinner, and must be perfect. Together they chose the menu: five courses ending in the traditional manner with fruit and finger-bowls handed round to each person. A few petals should be placed in each finger-bowl to decorate them, Mollie told the cook.

The guests arrived. Mollie and Hugh sat at opposite ends of the table, the colonel on Mollie's right, the colonel's lady next to Hugh, the others arranged in order of precedence. A series of stilted conversations began. Mollie took up her spoon and bent her head over her bowl of soup. Then she stared in consternation. Floating in the clear brown liquid were a number of red flower petals, tastefully arranged in a pattern. The same pattern decorated each bowl round the table.

She caught Hugh's eye and blushed furiously. Then she burst into laughter. 'Oh dear,' she cried. 'The cook must have misunderstood me.'

She looked so charming with her flushed face and rueful expression that everyone else laughed too.

'What a pity to spoil the pattern!' said the CO, smiling at her as he fished flower petals out of his soup.

Mollie's daily tasks of interviewing the *khitmagar* and the cook, walking round the grounds with the gardener and arranging flowers in the house were soon completed. Hugh left after breakfast, so she had most of the day to herself. She refused to waste it in social gossip with the other wives. She had braved the *moorghi-khana* and made some friends, but she did not want to be drawn into any of the cliques which existed in this rigidly defined white society.

Instead she wandered down the narrow paths on the hills around her house amidst the strange shrubs and trees, observing the Indian peasant women who strode up and down the steep slopes. Her professional eye noted their grace and poise. They were so sure-footed and strong, perfectly suited to their environment, balancing heavy tins of water brought up from the valley on their heads, or carrying children slung on their backs. They supported these weights with the minimum of effort, their muscles co-ordinated, their carriage upright.

We have to relearn what they know instinctively, she thought. Our civilized lives inhibit natural movement. We have to train our bodies afresh to be capable of it.

She was asked to start a class at the *moorghi-khana* and agreed, glad of this opportunity to continue her former work and adapt it to quite new conditions. She hoped that what she could teach the other wives would be useful to them. However, she stipulated that the small fees which her pupils paid should be sent to the Women's Social and Political Union in England. She had joined this suffragette organization during the last few years and was now, like all her sisters, a strong supporter of the women's cause. In the masculine stronghold of Lansdowne some eyebrows were raised at this, but Mollie persisted, even growing the words *Votes for Women* in one of her flower-beds.

Hugh took her to a favourite picnic place, called 'Tiffin-Top' by the English , situated on the peak of the highest local hill. A small, partly ruined temple stood there dedicated to Vishnu's daughter, flying a tattered flag with the god Shiva's trident inscribed on it. A cabbalistic sign was painted on the whitewashed wall below. Hugh told her that it represented *Om*, the sacred word of power intoned by yogis in their meditations.

'I wish I could speak the language better and learn something about the Hindu religion,' said Mollie.

'I'll try to find a teacher for you,' Hugh replied.

He remembered a phrase of yogic wisdom that he had heard when he first came to India. '*When you are ready to build you will find straw for your bricks.*'

Overlaid by so much since, these words sounded again in his mind. He found a *munshi*, an interpreter and teacher of languages, and Mollie's lessons began.

Mr Gopal was an elderly brahmin who wore a *dhoti* and steel-rimmed spectacles. His manner was gentle and reflective.

He never became irritated or impatient or raised his voice. Yet he had the power to dismiss inessentials and replace them with a benign concentration. Seated at a table, their books between them, he and Mollie would carry on a conversation in Urdu (she had already learnt some from Hugh), restricted on her side at first, but gradually becoming more confident and eloquent.

Hugh encouraged her. Sometimes in the evenings all three went for walks together. Led on by Hugh, Mr Gopal would talk to them about the Hindu view of life and the practice of yoga.

'It is a discipline which joins the body with the natural world; and the spirit with the universe, or cosmic consciousness,' he said. 'It is a long and dedicated training. First, you must educate the body through *asanas*, or right physical positions, which relate to balance and posture and affect the mind. Then, when mind and body have been attuned and purified, you may study the various rhythms of breathing, and these release the spirit.'

'So mind and body are closely related in yoga?' said Mollie.

'Certainly. There is no division.'

'Would it be possible to learn some of the *asanas*?'

Mr Gopal hesitated. He seemed to commune with himself for a moment before replying. Then he said, 'That would depend on your reason for wishing to do so.'

At the end of her next lesson Mollie told him of her interest in physical education and her training with Mrs Conn. Also of the way she had put this training into practice and gained good results with her pupils.

'The yoga *asanas* would give me a much deeper understanding of the relation of body and mind,' she explained. 'I feel that if I'm to go on with this work, the training of the body alone is not enough. It should be a means, not an end.'

'A means towards what?'

Mollie hesitated. With a touch of self-consciousness she replied, 'Towards illumination, or awareness, or greater insight – whatever you like to call it.'

This answer seemed to satisfy Mr Gopal. He arranged for a woman to come to the bungalow and instruct Mollie in some of the yoga *asanas* and relaxation techniques. Mollie took her lessons seriously and practised every day.

Hugh also expressed an interest in yoga philosophy. But Mr Gopal said to him, 'Sahib, you are a soldier. The karma of blood is blood. You have chosen your path. Contemplation may come in its own time, when you are as old as I.'

The autumn came with bright clear days in the hills and cold weather at last in the plains. Wives who had come up in the great heat of June departed to rejoin their husbands, and Lansdowne reverted to a small military station. Mollie and Hugh were able to spend more time together and less on social obligations.

She walked along the hill-paths with new life burgeoning all around her. Wild flowers covered the slopes, fields of corn ripened, mists lifted from the mountains. Within her, too, life quickened. A baby would be born in the early summer of next year. The landscape seemed to reflect her joy.

Mollie had none of the fear and misgivings often associated with pregnancy. Her body was already trained and she knew how to prepare for the ultimate test of a woman's physique – successful childbirth. Mrs Conn's insistence on breathing techniques and the correct training of the abdominal and pelvic muscles now stood her in good stead. She practised her yoga *asanas* and relaxation every day and continued teaching her classes until two months before her confinement.

In early May 1913, Mollie's baby was born. It was a boy. As soon as her labour started she entered the small hospital in Lansdowne and was attended by the resident doctor, who delivered the baby, and the nurses there. Everything went according to plan; both mother and child were in good health. The proud parents chose the name Peter for their son (Peter had been Hugh's nickname for many years) and cabled their respective families. But their happiness was tragically short-lived. Within a week their baby had died.

Many babies died in India. Their poignant gravestones in the cemeteries of British churches were a familiar sight. Conditions in the small hospitals of remote hill-stations like Lansdowne were unpredictable. Peter had been a robust child at birth, but somehow he contracted a severe infection and died almost straight away.

Mollie said afterwards that with his death real sorrow entered her life. She could not believe that her happiness would ever again be unshadowed. Her responsive body which had stood the test of childbirth so well was now bereft of its fulfilment. She could not reconcile herself to the loss. The months of preparation, her confidence and optimism, all now seemed in vain.

Then one day Mr Gopal called. He offered his condolences and sat at a respectful distance, hands folded in his lap, eyes focused above her head, spectacles gleaming.

There was silence between them. Mollie felt some of her tension dissolving. He began to talk to her in a quiet voice.

'Your little son has been taken from you,' he said, 'and this is hard for you, because he was within your body and had entered your spirit. But if you can accept his physical loss you will see that he is part now of the cosmic consciousness which you yourself are trying to reach through your yoga training.'

'I miss him so. It was such a cruel, sudden cutting-off.'

'It seems so. But in reality nothing ends. All is transmuted into a different existence, just as this year's fallen leaves make next year's flowers.'

'I feel so bereft.'

'You have the memory of growing life within you. You cannot dictate what will happen to that life when it enters the world. You can only accept its karma, its fate. You have your husband's love.'

Mollie nodded. Through the open window came the scent of roses. She remembered her arrival in Lansdowne a year ago, roses blooming in the evening light, Hugh's proud face. . . .

Mr Gopal dropped his gaze from the ceiling, adjusted his spectacles, and met her tearful eyes. 'Together you will make another child,' he said.

Mollie was now an Indian Army wife of a year's standing. During that time she had learnt much about Hugh's regiment and his attitude to his men.

The 2nd Battalion, 8th Gurkhas had been raised in Assam in 1872, though there had been Gurkha regiments since 1815. This eastern frontier of India, bordered by China, Tibet and

Burma, provided almost unceasing active service for the soldiers protecting it. Its capital was Shillong, where Hugh's father and stepfather had served in the Indian Civil Service and where Hugh himself had been born. His battalion was based there but had been transferred to Lansdowne in May 1906, where he had joined it six months later.

The Gurkha soldiers were strong small hillmen, Mongolian in origin, famous for their courage and endurance. They were recruited from Nepal and served as mercenaries, not subjects of the British Crown. Nevertheless, they gave it unstinting loyalty, remaining steadfast during the Indian Mutiny, and dying on many foreign fields for the British cause.

They were commanded by British and Gurkha officers and there were close ties between them.

'Rely on your Gurkha officers,' Hugh was told when he joined the regiment as a young second lieutenant and discovered that not only was he expected to command a whole company, but that he would be the only British officer in it.

A Gurkha battalion was a family affair. The traditions were passed on from soldier father to soldier son. The British officers all spoke Gurkhali, understood and admired their men and felt responsible for their welfare.

'It's like a sort of exclusive club,' Mollie explained to Nan, who had come out to India to be with her after Peter's death. 'The whole station revolves round the regiment and its traditions.'

'Don't you find that too limiting?' asked Nan.

'I did at first. Now I've adapted to it. India itself is so fascinating. And I have Hugh.'

Mollie arranged a dinner-party for Nan.

'The CO, Colonel Murray, is coming', she told her, 'with his wife. They're nice but very conventional. I hope you'll like them.'

At dinner the colonel sat next to Mollie and opened the conversation. 'How does your garden grow?' he teased her.

'Very well, thank you. My sister approves of one bed in particular.'

'I can guess which one. She's a keen suffragette, too, isn't she?'

'Certainly.'

The colonel turned to Nan, sitting on his other side. 'Tell me the latest news about the women's movement at home.'

Nan was looking her best that evening. Her ruby-red dress enhanced her white skin. Her dark hair was piled on top of her head, held by a ribbon and a flower. Her eyes were brilliant. She gave the colonel an innocent smile.

'I'm so glad you're interested in it,' she replied. 'We all are, too. My younger sister Charlotte has just been carted off to prison in a Black Maria.'

'Good heavens!' exclaimed the colonel. 'What did she do?'

'She knocked a policeman's helmet off his head and kicked him on the shins.'

The colonel's eyes bulged. 'Why?' he rasped.

Nan continued to smile sweetly. 'The women's movement has entered a militant phase,' she explained. 'The government wouldn't listen to reason, so now the suffragettes have to use force. My sister was obeying orders. As a military man you must understand that.'

The colonel's face deepened in colour.

On his other side, Mollie said, 'No one likes violence. But the women have been driven to it. Now they're hunger-striking in prison and being forcibly fed. It's a war.'

The colonel turned from one pair of earnest eyes to the other. He took a deep breath. 'My dear young ladies,' he proclaimed. 'I understand a war. But this one is unnecessary. The women don't *have* to break the law. They don't *have* to smash windows and be put in prison. They don't even *have* to have the vote. They can control their men perfectly well without it. As they always have.'

Nan's eye caught Hugh's at the top of the table. With her scarlet cheeks she looked like a warrior, but for her hosts' sake she decided to retreat.

'Perhaps you're right,' she countered. 'Anyway, that's certainly the best policy for a masculine stronghold like this. I promise you I'll conform to it for as long as I'm here.'

Nan's visit continued with picnics, dances, rides and

supper-parties and ended with her giving a song recital at the
club. She chose a programme which would not unduly tax her
voice or her audience.

'She sings charmingly,' the colonel whispered to his wife.

But Nan could not resist announcing that she would finish
her recital with the Irish irredentist song, 'The Wearing of the
Green'.

Hugh shifted apprehensively in his seat. What was coming
now, he wondered?

> Oh! Paddy dear, an' did you hear the news that be goin'
>   round?
> The shamrock is forbid by law to grow on Irish ground!
> Saint Patrick's Day no more we'll keep, his colour can't be
>   seen,
> For there's a cruel law agin' the wearin' of the
>   green! . . .
> She's the most distressful country that ever yet was seen,
> For they're hangin' men and women there for wearin' of
>   the green.

The next day Nan left. Hugh, returning to Mollie after
escorting her down the hillside to the railhead, sank into a chair
and mopped his brow with relief.

In October Hugh obtained a short leave and took Mollie into
the hills for a ten-day trek. A number of Gurkhas accompanied
them. Hugh's bearer was in charge of the camp, assisted by a
cook, two Gurkha soldier servants and several porters who
carried the loads. Treks in the hills were a familiar part of
Lansdowne life. The Gurkhas enjoyed them as much as their
sahibs and maintained high standards of service. Mollie
expected some discomfort, but except for the natural physical
tiredness after a long day she was as well looked after on the trek
as in her own home.

The regions round Lansdowne, as far as the Himalayan
frontier, were populated by the Garhwal tribe from which men
were recruited for the Garhwal Rifles, the other Lansdowne
regiment. It had been stationed there since 1887. As with the

Gurkhas in Nepal, most of the villages through which Hugh and Mollie passed had supplied men for the Garhwal regiment, often for several generations back. Hugh and his Gurkhas were greeted by these veterans with delight, and Mollie was shown souvenirs of service – medals, rifles, uniforms – and told stories of battles, translated by Hugh.

Each day they covered new ground. They walked along narrow paths on ridges, descended steeply into valleys, climbed up to further hilltops, traversed more spines. They looked back over longer and longer distances to their starting-point. But however far they travelled they seemed to draw no nearer to the great Himalayas, shining on the northern horizon; ethereal, untouchable, revealing themselves from the clouds at sunset or dawn.

The Gurkhas marched ahead. When they arrived in the late afternoon at the night's camping place, all was prepared. Tents had been erected – a sleeping-tent, a mess-tent and a store-tent – a fire was lit between large stones and tea was made. Sometimes then Hugh would leave Mollie while he went out with a rifle to shoot game for the pot. She would slip off her boots, stretch out her tired legs and sit by the fire, joking with the cook while he prepared the evening meal and told her the news of the day.

All around were the foothills of the mountains, a territory shared with Indian chamois, Indian roe deer, black bear and hill *sambur* stag. There were also wild goats and wild sheep, or, more perilously, an occasional leopard. Hugh had shot a tiger in these hills when he first came to Lansdowne. He put out a kill to lure the beast, camped all night in a tree to watch out for it, and then shot it.

At night the air was crisp and the fire leapt and flickered, sending up showers of sparks when fresh logs were thrown on it. The smell of deodar wood, the warmth of the flames and the touch of each other stirred Hugh's and Mollie's senses as they sat close together, backs to the darkness beyond. Sometimes they sang; sometimes they listened to the Gurkhas singing and telling stories. Sometimes they lay full length and gazed up at the bright stars, watching the constellations that swung slowly across the sky. Somewhere there would be a sound of water, a sound of wind rustling through leaves, the last call of a bird.

And somewhere far away in darkness stood the Himalayan giants, mountain upon mountain, invisible, impregnable, guarding the frontier.

They woke before dawn, the cook bringing them hot sweet tea and warm washing water. They struggled out of their sleeping-bags and into their clothes and stumbled outside to clean their teeth. And then the sun rose, heralded by a pink glow on the topmost peaks, deepening and spreading until the whole range was illuminated and on fire. Another day's trek began.

Mollie grew fit, sunburnt and strong. Her depression about her lost baby dissolved. She felt completely at home in this environment and deeply happy, and her happiness grew every day. The sun streamed down from a cloudless sky, its heat tempered by the autumn season. The clarity of the air reflected the clarity of her emotions. Here with Hugh, in the hills they both loved, she wanted nothing more of life.

Mollie never forgot those days. Afterwards, she looked back on them as the most precious and perfect in her life.

Billy Luttman-Johnson, Hugh's half-brother, and his junior by seven years, came to stay. He had recently joined the 9th Bengal Lancers (Hodson's Horse) and this was his first leave.

Hugh welcomed him warmly and introduced Mollie.

'I'd have known you by the family resemblance,' she said. 'You look like Hugh. Welcome to our home.'

Billy bent down to kiss her. What a corker of a girl Hugh has chosen! he thought to himself.

He and Hugh had long talks about the rival merits of Pathans and Gurkhas and of their respective regiments.

'You're so lucky to be in a fixed hill-station, with a permanent mess,' said Billy. 'I envy you all the sport in the hills around.'

'I know,' Hugh replied. 'But we do get a bit cut off up here, miles from the nearest railhead. You're more in touch in the plains. What's the latest news from home?'

'Troubles with the Irish and the suffragettes.'

'Yes. Mollie's sister Nan brought us up to date on all that.

But I'd like to know about the military situation. Are we heading for war with Germany?'

Billy sat forward in his chair, elbows on his knees. 'I hope not, Hugh. But it looks uncommonly like it. The Germans have been trying to match our fleet as fast as they can.'

'What's the Admiralty view?'

'Churchill and Lord Fisher have decided to create a Fast Division with battleships fuelled by oil which are capable of great speed. It's a revolutionary concept. They'll cost over three million pounds each. The Admiralty are all for it, but the Cabinet are jibbing at the expense.'

'I hope it'll go through. Naval strength is vital for our supplies. But if there is a war, the decisive battles will be fought out on land in Europe.'

'I suppose so. If France is attacked by Germany we'd certainly go to her aid.'

'It would involve more than ourselves and France. The Austro-Hungarian Empire would come in to support Germany, Russia to support France, probably the Dominions to support us, certainly India. . . . Do you think people in England really expect all this to happen?'

'I don't know. Service people like ourselves are preparing. But I doubt if the average person sees the danger, in spite of the Kaiser's posturing.'

'If it comes, it will be overwhelming,' said Hugh. 'Not something like the Boer War or the campaigns fought here by professional soldiers. It will involve everyone, the whole world.'

Billy raised his face to Hugh. His eyes shone with excitement. 'We'd be in the thick of it,' he said. 'It's what we've been trained for, what our regiments exist for. What an adventure!'

Hugh was silent. He stared at the ground, his whole frame tense. As if to himself, he murmured, '*The karma of blood is blood.*'

Billy proved to be a less controversial guest than Nan. He spent most of his time out of doors, shooting in the hills, climbing and trekking. He accompanied Mollie on her mountain walks and she found him a delightful companion.

'Hugh's ideally suited to this life,' he told her. 'He's a born

leader. He speaks Gurkhali expertly and his men love him.
He'll go far in the Indian Army, you wait and see!'

Mollie laughed, amused at this authoritative pronounce-
ment from a younger brother. She was sorry when Billy's leave
ended.

In January 1914 the regiment moved to the plains for
manoeuvres. Mollie and the other wives were left behind in
Lansdowne while the men marched south. The foothills were
covered in snow. The sun rose on a bare landscape. By day it
often shone from a cloudless sky, but when it set the night
became bitterly cold. Bundles of hay, stored in trees for winter
cattle-feed, were brought down and given to hungry beasts.
Rice in the fields shrivelled to barren stalks.

Mollie was pregnant. Another baby was on the way and
would be born next July. Now that she was alone she had plenty
of time to think and dream. She still went for her walks each day
and regarded them as a kind of vigil. Years later, she wrote:

> When my child began, I hoped – what I imagine that nine
> out of ten mothers hope, and so I dare to write it down – I
> hoped that my coming child would be good and beautiful,
> and somehow great. But knowing that we were both fairly
> ordinary parents, I became ashamed of the egoism of these
> presumptuous thoughts. Yet, day after day, back came the
> thought insistently: 'My baby must be beautiful.' The good
> and great idea I eliminated, because I knew that the
> magnetic beauty I wanted must result in these two as well.
>
> So every day I thought of this beauty and hoped, but also
> every day I became more conscious of my own mediocrity,
> and despaired. One day, standing on a lovely hillside, gazing
> enraptured at the magnificent beauty of the sun setting over
> the distant Himalayas, their great hunched shoulders
> blanketed with warm snow – for the sunset lit them with
> every glowing colour from vermilion to palest pink – all the
> tension of uncertain longing within me broke, my spirit
> relaxed, and a thrilling worship of the beauty before me
> flooded my whole being. . . . I realized why Greek artists
> found that they had daily to turn again and 'bathe in

Nature'; why the beauty of an ancient urn thrilled the poet Keats to his burst of religious ecstasy: ' "Beauty is truth, truth beauty," – that is all/ Ye know on earth, and all ye need to know.'

The little thoughts of self and my own mediocrity, spelling egoism and so failure, were drowned in the flood of feeling that the scene around me inspired. Suddenly I understood the two forms of humility – the one that despises and belittles oneself, and the other which, *self-forgetting, worships something great.* At last I seemed to sense why Jesus began his sermon: 'Blessed are the *poor in spirit,* for theirs is the Kingdom of Heaven.' From that day I saw that Beauty was the Kingdom of Heaven, the abode of God, the *thing* that we small humans must worship if we are to attain insight and power.

Day after day, month after month, I returned to that spot full of faith in the future. . . . *

Mollie's faith was justified. Spring came, then summer. Near the end of it, on a day when the rains had temporarily ceased, she was walking with Hugh in the garden, rain-washed yet bathed in summer sunshine. She felt her birth-pangs begin. She went indoors, for this time she was having her baby at home. The doctor was called at once but arrived almost too late. Throughout her short labour Mollie remembered the medley of brightly coloured flowers which she had just seen, fresh and opening to the sun, and felt that this impression must influence her child. Her baby was born within half an hour – a girl whom they called Prunella. The doctor pronounced her in perfect health. The date was 28 July 1914.

On this same day, in distant Europe, Austria declared war on Serbia. It was the first step towards the mobilization of the armies of the world. Its outcome was the Great War.

---

* Mary Bagot Stack, *Building the Body Beautiful.*

5

The Karma of Blood

All that summer of 1914, tension had been mounting in Europe. After Austria had declared war on Serbia, Russia, Germany and then France mobilized and Britain put her fleet on a war footing. Germany delivered a demand to Belgium to allow German troops free passage through Belgian territory. Belgium refused. Germany then declared war on France and her army streamed across the Belgian border. Finally, during the last hours of Tuesday, 4 August, Britain's ultimatum to Germany to respect Belgium's neutrality expired. Peace was at an end.

Twenty minutes later a historic War Telegram was dispatched to all corners of the Empire. It read, 'War, Germany, Act.'

In Lansdowne, Hugh and Mollie had had one week of unclouded happiness with their new baby. Then war was declared. Hugh's Gurkha battalion was ordered into action. It would sail for an unknown destination as soon as it could be made ready.

Mollie felt the destructiveness of war with every fibre of her being, but she realized that she had married a soldier and she must accept the consequences. Her baby's birth had brought her close to the creative processes of life. War was the exact opposite. Hugh and his fellow officers were trained to resist an aggressor, to defend their country with patriotism. Mollie could think only of the immense waste and tragedy that war would bring to the world.

Hugh told her the facts he knew. They would be parted almost immediately and she would have to travel back to England alone. He would soon be involved in the fighting. They might not hear news of each other for many weeks. He did not minimize the danger or the seriousness of what lay ahead. In those last days they were able to share their feelings and draw strength from one another; there were no barriers between them.

The battalion was one of the first in the Indian Army to be sent overseas. Speed in equipping it for active service was essential. Hugh, now a Captain, was occupied all day. He was concerned also with the personal problems of his men. In the Gurkha tradition of family involvement, they sought his help and advice.

Mollie, too, was busy. She had to see to the preparation of Hugh's kit, choose what he should take, and try to imagine what would be of most comfort and use to him. Every object was poignant. It would be the only link between them when he unpacked. And who knew where that would be? Although the battalion sailed under sealed orders, everyone guessed that its destination was France.

The last evening came. Hugh and Mollie walked round the garden together and then went from room to room in the house. They were both exhausted. Mollie had a severe headache. Hugh's nerves were strung tight. Prunella lay asleep in her cot. Hugh bent over her, touching her cheek and murmuring 'Goodbye.' There seemed nothing more to say.

The next day, 21 August, reveille sounded at first light. The battalion assembled on the parade-ground, ready to march down the mountain path to the railhead. The Gurkhas stood to attention, brown faces impassive, uniforms spotless, equipment gleaming. The officers were mounted, each in front of his men. The Gurkha pipes tuned up. The march began.

Hugh turned his horse up the hill and halted in front of his bungalow to say goodbye. Mollie was waiting for him, shading her eyes against the rising sun. They kissed. He rode away and she heard the wail of the pipes and the sound of tramping feet. She watched until his white horse disappeared round a bend, then she raised her eyes to the morning sky. The far hills were

touched with rosy light. She gazed at them, seeking strength
and comfort. Instead, in a great arch across the sky, she saw the
words: *Riding to his death.*

She knew these words were true.

The battalion travelled by train to Karachi. Now that they had
left their hill-station, the Gurkhas responded to the excitement
of the journey with their usual zest. They were natural
combatants, keen to be in action. They accepted Britain's war
with fatalism and were determined to let nothing stop them
from getting into the thick of it as soon as possible. At the
railhead one of Hugh's riflemen caught his hand in a carriage
door as it slammed. His little finger was badly injured. Fearing
that he might be left behind, he quickly unsheathed his *kukri*
and cut the finger off. This action was typical.

Very few of these Gurkhas had seen anything but Nepal, the
hill-depots where they were trained, and the plains where
manoeuvres took place. They had never been out of India.
Special permission had to be secured from the Raj Guru,
Nepal's supreme religious authority, for them to cross the *kala
pani* (black water), for Hindus were forbidden to do this on pain
of loss of caste. They would have to take part in a purification
ceremony – the *pani patiya* – when they returned; but as
mercenary troops they were allowed to go.

The battalion reached Karachi full of confidence and
excitement, and became part of the Bareilly Brigade of the
Meerut Division (7th), embarking on BISS *Erinpura* and sailing
in a convoy of thirty-two ships, escorted by the Royal Navy, the
Royal Indian Marine and, at a later stage, ships of the French
Fleet.

The Gurkhas encountered the sea for the first time. They
were hillmen, used to mountains, not to rolling waves and
fathomless water. Did the ship run on rails at the bottom of the
sea? one asked. How, otherwise, could it find its way? Another,
hanging over the deck-rail, explained that he was trying to see
the ship's legs. They were all uneasy on the water and most
succumbed to seasickness.

The voyage was long – between six and seven weeks. Hugh,
after the wrench of departure at Lansdowne and the bustle of

embarking at Karachi, had plenty of time to think. He tried to picture leading his men into action. What would it be like in France? How would they adapt to unknown conditions? This was just such a crisis for which he and they had long been trained. He had no doubts of their courage or loyalty. Would he be able to live up to the expectations they had of him as their leader? Whatever happened, Hugh for his part hoped they would all do their duty. Duty and honour were words that must be turned into deeds.

While Hugh was embarking at Karachi and sailing towards Port Said and Marseilles, the French and British armies were fighting a desperate action. The Germans had swept across Belgium and forced the Allies to retreat all along the Western Front. Paris was in peril, as more and more French territory was yielded.

Then came the 'miracle of the Marne'. The French, so near disaster, staked all in a final stand. General Joffre, the Commander-in-Chief, gave the order: 'A unit which finds it impossible to advance must, regardless of cost, hold its ground and be killed on the spot rather than fall back.' Every available man was thrown into battle. The line held and the French offensive forced the German armies back. The British, with their four divisions, gave vital support on the extreme left flank. And on 5 September the Battle of the Marne was won. The Germans were halted.

They were still in possession of all Belgium and all of northern France as far as the Aisne. Reinforcements were sorely needed. The Indian Army Corps were thrown immediately into the front line. Trained for the defence of India, they had no experience of the type of warfare which would be demanded of them in France. They were rushed into waterlogged trenches, subjected to constant bombardment and outnumbered in German attacks by seven to one. But they held on.

Lord Harding, Viceroy of India, later summed up their heroism:

It is to the abiding glory of the Indian Corps that it reached

France in the first great crisis of the war. The only trained
reinforcements immediately available in any part of the
Empire arrived in time to stem the German thrust towards
Ypres and the Channel ports during the autumn of 1914.
They consecrated with their blood the unity of India with the
Empire: and few indeed are the survivors of that gallant
force.

With Hugh gone, Mollie was left without news. She heard that
the battalion had embarked at Karachi and knew that they
must be sailing to France. Every day put a wider stretch of
ocean between herself and Hugh. Her vision of the words *Riding
to his death* remained with her. She could not explain it and tried
to banish it from her everyday life. It sank to the realm of
dreams and the unconscious. But she knew there that it was
true.

In Lansdowne, only a skeleton military structure of the
Gurkhas' base remained. Most of the Gurkha wives were
advised to return to Nepal, for no one knew for how long their
husbands would be away. Mollie visited them, hoping to
console them and found, instead of tears, a stoic acceptance of
their fate. Coming from a country of poverty, privation and
natural disasters, they were used to catastrophe.

Mollie felt ashamed of her self-centred grief. Her courage
and resilience returned. All the British wives were in the same
position as herself. They were closing up their houses and
trying to secure a passage on a ship home as soon as possible.
With the battalion gone, life in Lansdowne had suddenly
become unreal.

At last the day came when they could leave. The reveille
bugle sounded at dawn, as on the morning of Hugh's
departure. Mollie woke, ran to her window and leant out. The
sky was touched with mysterious light. On the horizon,
disembodied and ethereal, floating like a bank of fragile clouds,
were the Himalayas. Their mantle of snow deepened to rose.
Bare-footed in her nightdress, Mollie gazed at them, trying to
imprint on her memory each form and shape of distant beauty.

Whatever happens to my world, she thought, those
mountains will remain.

She knew she would never see them again.

The journey down the hillside to the railhead was unbearable, with its evocation of the ride she and Hugh had taken in the opposite direction. It was a relief to reach Karachi and the ship. The docks hummed with the activity of regiments embarking for service overseas. The Indian troops were fatalistic, the British excited at the prospect of Home and War. The two words, at present linked together in their minds, were soon to be pulled roughly apart.

The long sea voyage began. Mollie tried to banish its end from her mind and live for each day, caring for her baby in the great heat which caught up with them in the Red Sea, helping the other mothers and children, most of whom were suffering from minor illnesses.

Hugh was somewhere ahead of her on the ocean. He had started out about three weeks before. Leaning over the deck-rail in the evening, she watched the moon's reflection on the water. Was he watching too? The night's beauty was far removed from war, but war was what both of them were sailing towards. All round her people were preparing themselves to face the ordeal. Hugh, too, must be preparing himself. Perhaps he was trying to put his family out of his mind and to shut out poignant memories. He would need all his strength and single-minded dedication for what he had to do.

The battalion reached Marseilles on 13 October. They disembarked amid an animated scene. Dashing uniforms of French colonial troops – Algerians and Zouaves – mixed with sober British khaki. French seamen and stevedores helped the Gurkhas unload. Though they spoke no one else's language, the friendliness and humour of the Nepalese hillmen soon communicated itself with signs and gestures. They collected their kit and marched off to their camp.

During the next few days they went for route marches in the surrounding countryside. They were delighted to be on terra firma again, but confusing impressions assailed them at every step. Where was the clear bright light of India? The sunshine was muted, sending beams through clouds or disappearing altogether in an overcast sky. On the roads there were no slow ox-carts; there was no time for people to stop to exchange the gossip of the day. In the villages massive stone buildings with spires contained the white man's God. There were no mountains, and no mountain shrines. They felt a yearning for their hills.

They were issued with new rifles and by 18 October were ready to march off again north to their advance base, which they reached three days later. Here they stayed for five days, joined by a much-needed French interpreter. At the same time, the billeting party were supplied with bicycles. This was a source of great amusement to men who had never ridden bicycles before. But carefree days were almost over. On 26 October the battalion went by train to Lillers and then marched to Gorre, just behind the front line. It was two weeks since they had landed in France.

They were now within artillery range of the enemy. The march to Gorre had been long and tedious, and on arrival there they hoped for a rest and something to eat. But they were urgently needed in the front line. There was no time to prepare them for conditions in the trenches and no commissariat to produce a meal. After a few hours they were hurried on again.

At this time the Indian Army corps was holding nine miles of the British front line in the La Bassée-Festubert-Neuve Chapelle area. They were there from the beginning of October 1914 until the spring of 1915. There had no reserves to back them up and suffered very heavy casualties. Gurkha regiments played a gallant part in this defence, but at a great cost. They lost the majority of their British officers, and this loss was irreplaceable, for only these officers knew the men intimately, spoke their language and understood their background and traditions. When Hugh's battalion was ordered to take over trenches near Festubert, they were helping to release men for the defence of Ypres, a battle vital for the safety of the Channel ports.

The Gurkha riflemen, however, marching up the dreary road to the front line, knew nothing of this higher strategy. Tired and hungry, they were receiving their baptism of shell-fire. All around them was low-lying land, broken up by numerous lanes and streams. This had been an area of cultivated fields, small villages and isolated farms. But already the few trees had been reduced to skeletal stumps and many of the buildings to crumbling walls. In winter all would become a sea of mud. The Gurkhas, peering through the murky fog, could discern only a stricken landscape where nothing lived.

The battalion moved into position that evening, 29 October. Its whole strength was up in the front line. Half of each company were sent into a forward dug trench. The remainder occupied a ditch along a road. Hugh's company was in the right sector of one of the forward trenches.

These trenches, only eighty yards from the German lines, had been hastily constructed by the previous British battalion in face of constant shelling and rifle fire. They afforded some protection, but were too deep for the Gurkhas who were not tall enough to fire over the parapet. So their first task, in the cold and mud, was to build up the floor of the trench so that they could see their enemy.

The night dragged past, accompanied by the rumble of artillery fire and livid lights cast into the sky. No one slept. Soon after dawn the next day, the Germans attacked. They were beaten off, to be replaced with hours of shelling, culminating in a four-hour concentration of heavy guns and howitzers. The trenches became channels of death.

All telephone wires had been cut and there was no communication. The Gurkhas held on, nevertheless, and drove back several more attacks, mounting counter-attacks in return. Ammunition began to run low.

The forward companies suffered very heavy losses. Hours of continual shelling deafened the men. Dead and dying lay heaped around them. They were completely unused to such warfare. The enemy, with far greater fire-power, were decimating them from a distance with no possibility of an answering attack. Standing precariously on their makeshift platforms, reaching up to the parapet, those who were still alive tried to return fire.

The Germans had occupied a farmhouse on the right of the forward trenches. Snipers could fire from there and pick off British officers, who were dressed differently from their men. They also commanded the ground over which reinforcements could advance.

Realizing the danger, Hugh made his way along the trenches

towards the farmhouse, rallying his men and telling them there was nothing to fear. He had been hit twice, once in the cheek and once in the left arm. No British officer was unwounded. Hugh was heard to say, 'I don't know what we shall do if we cannot get the men to cover themselves better.'

Then suddenly he realized that the trench was surrounded. The enemy had broken through on the right and taken the defenders in the rear. Hugh drew his revolver from its holster. The Germans stormed on. Their numbers were overwhelming – five to one. Hugh stood steadfast, firing his revolver. Then he was hit again – this time fatally in the chest. He fell to the ground.

The Germans fixed their bayonets and charged. All was chaos. Men fought hand to hand in the mêlée, half in, half out of the trenches. The surviving Gurkhas were forced back. Eventually they succeeded in reaching a sector of their own support line, but all the forward trenches had to be abandoned. The killed and wounded disappeared, many of them buried by shell-fire.

The battalion suffered terribly. In one day's engagement 9 British officers, 5 Gurkha officers and 206 NCOs and riflemen were killed, wounded or missing. The British officer losses were a crippling blow.

'The 8th Gurkhas,' wrote Lieutenant-Colonel Mereweather in his book *The Indian Corps in France* of 1917, 'were fortunate in embarking in this war in possession of a particularly fine body of officers, and it was by the cruellest of bad luck that the Regiment at the very outset suffered the loss of no less than nine of their small number.'

On the next day, 31 October, the battalion was relieved by the Leicestershire Regiment. Dazed and exhausted, the men marched back to Gorre, leaving on the battlefield nearly two hundred of their strength.

They were not the only Gurkha battalion to suffer. Others were soon heavily engaged. Within a few days in early November, one lost all its British officers, and after a week in the trenches at Givenchy, another was reduced to half its strength.

Aboard the ship on the high seas, Mollie was sealed off from events in France and had no knowledge of the Gurkhas' ordeal. After the oppressive heat of the Red Sea, the Mediterranean was a relief. At last they were steaming into European waters.

The convoy passed through the Straits of Gibraltar, sailed up the coast of Spain and entered the Bay of Biscay. There it was hit by a powerful storm. All through the voyage the danger of submarines and the fear of their attack had haunted the passengers. Now they were subjected to the violence of nature instead. The ship tossed and rolled, creaked ominously, reared up on the crest of a wave and clapped down into its trough. Spray bombarded the portholes; objects clattered around the cabin; decks were awash.

The convoy became scattered, and some time elapsed before it was collected together again. At last it steamed on towards England, and finally berthed at Plymouth on 17 November, several days late.

While waiting to disembark, a friend of Mollie's slipped ashore to telephone their families. Mollie and the baby were left on their own. Newspapers were brought on board and she seized one. It was full of news that she longed to read, but she turned at once to the casualty lists. They were appallingly long. How could so many be killed, wounded or missing? She scanned them hurriedly. Suddenly one name leapt out at her, hitting her like a physical blow.

Stack. Edward Hugh Bagot, Captain. 2/8th Gurkha Rifles. Killed in action, October 30.

That was over two weeks before! Hugh had died and she had gone on living. It was impossible. How could she not have known? The newspaper slid from her hands and a black tide engulfed her. But even in that moment of despair Mollie realized that she *had* known. She had always known. This was the price of their happiness. Hugh had been taken, and nothing could ever be the same again.

Nan had come to meet her to break the news of Hugh's loss. The sisters travelled back to London together on the long train

journey from Plymouth. Beyond the window, the trees were
bare. Leafless branches made stark patterns against the winter
sky. Darkness fell. Nan drew down the carriage blinds. She
brought Mollie tea, arranged a rug over her knees, and took her
hand. But Mollie stayed silent all the way. The only thing that
roused her was a cry or movement from her baby.

At last they reached London. The train pulled in at Waterloo
Station. Norah and their mother met them, found a porter and
took them outside. It was raining. They stood in a queue
waiting for a cab and Mollie saw spears of rain streaming across
the lights of the traffic, glistening on leaves, blurring the
street-lamps and spitting into reflections on the wet roads. She
heard the rain's soft patter and turned to Nan.

'This is just how Hugh and I always imagined London,' she
said. 'In the rain. With the lamps huge and indistinct and the
lights reflected in the streets. We always thought it would look
like this when we came home together.'

She clasped her baby tightly. 'Prunella feels so heavy,' she
said.

At the flat her mother had rented a letter awaited Mollie.

'It's from France,' Charlotte said. 'Don't read it yet, darling.
I didn't open it. I left it for you. But rest a little while before you
look at it.'

Mollie held out her hand for the letter, took it and slit the
envelope. She drew out a sheet of paper. 'It's from Major
Cassels,' she said. She began to read it.

We got into the firing trenches on the night of 29/30 October.
The 30th was the awful day. The Germans attacked heavily
on our right and your husband was killed. The only details I
have been able to collect were that your husband was first hit
in the cheek by a rifle bullet. He could not speak much but
asked his Subadar for a cigarette which the Subadar gave
him. When he had smoked it he got up and went along the
trenches to the right urging the men to fire and saying there
was nothing to fear. Subsequently he was hit again in the left
arm, but that did not deter him from fighting on, and when
the enemy advanced he was standing up and shooting with
his revolver when he was hit a third time. This struck him in
the chest and must have killed him instantaneously for he

never moved again.

Besides your husband we lost killed that day Major Wake, Captains Sadler, Wright and Hartwell. Missing, Captain Davidson. Wounded, Colonel Morris, Major Barlow and Lieutenant Maclean. Only Captain Buckland and myself came out of action untouched.

Mollie put the letter carefully back into its envelope and handed it to Nan.

'You tell them,' she said. Then she pushed away the cups and plates in front of her on the tea-table and laid her arms and head there. Great shudders shook her body from head to foot. They did not cease until her mother knelt beside her and enfolded her in her arms.

Hugh's half-brother Billy had arrived in France from India a week before and Rosalie, his mother, wrote to him there. She told him of the Gurkhas' ordeal and Hugh's death, and added:

Mollie arrived in London last Tuesday – I saw her on Wednesday. Poor, poor girl, it is terrible, she was very broken and desolate. Hugh was everything to her, and to arrive only to hear this. . . . May and I were with her as much as possible for the first two days. To-day she is *much* better and calmer and beginning to get a grip on herself, as I know how strong and brave she is. Her mother has taken a flat for a time and Mollie is with her. Later on they will live together I think, probably in London, but we can make no plans yet.

Rosalie's affection, and the knowledge that she shared Hugh's loss as no one else could, were a great help to Mollie during the first dark days. The barrier which had lain between them dissolved. But Rosalie seemed able to accept Hugh's death more philosophically than her daughter-in-law. Mollie still felt acutely conscious of the horror of war. She imagined every detail of the Gurkhas' action, lived it within herself and tried to share Hugh's ordeal.

'And we're only at the beginning,' she said to Nan.

The sisters were sitting before a coal-fire, snug and warm, indulging in their first long talk together since her return.

'Just think of the conditions in the trenches now that winter has set in. Mud, floods, disease, acute discomfort, quite apart from continual danger. And it may go on for years. Years of waste and loss. For what?'

Nan found it hard to answer. 'Those officers in your regiment,' she said at last, 'they seemed to know what they would be fighting for. Their country, home, liberty . . . '

'Of course. Hugh felt the same. They had no choice. They were soldiers and they had to fight. And we'll have to support the war now till it's over. But oh! Nan, the casualties. . . '

'People are appalled by them. Those awful lists. The troop trains coming back from France crowded with the wounded. We'll have to help in some way.'

'Norah's going to join the women's service – the WAACs. She's the right age for it. She'll enjoy it. But I can't do anything like that. I have to look after Prunella.'

'Thank God you have her. It'll give you a reason for living.'

'I know. But she can't make up for Hugh's loss.' Mollie clasped her hands, and gazed at her sister, her grief naked in her eyes. 'How am I going to bear the next few years, Nan? How can I live without hope?'

Nan leant forward to poke the fire. It blazed up and coloured her serious face. She lifted her head and turned to Mollie.

'Without hope perhaps, Mollie, but not without faith,' she said. 'You *had* your two years with Hugh. Remember that. You were given more happiness than many people know in a lifetime. Have faith in the future.'

'You sound like my yoga teacher in India,' said Mollie. 'Accept your fate. It's true, of course, but very, very hard to do when you've lost what matters most to you in the world.' She paused. 'Oh, Nan, what a long way we've come since we used to pour out our hearts to each other in our little room at Blackrock!'

'We've grown up. We know now that life's hard, and full of terrible events. We can't deceive ourselves any more.'

Mollie detected a poignant note in her sister's voice. Perhaps Nan, too, had her losses. She leant forward and laid her hand on her sister's knee. 'We'll help each other,' she said.

Each evening Mollie put Prunella to bed with a special ritual. After the bath the baby sat on her knee, freshly washed and dressed in a long nightgown, and Mollie sang to her. Then she placed her in her cot and sat beside her until Prunella fell asleep.

Often, during these moments of vigil, she thought of Lansdowne. She longed to preserve her memories of it intact, but already they were fading. London, with its black-out, its khaki crowds, its mixture of hectic pleasures and terrible realities, was blotting them out. How could she remember the beauty of the Himalayas when war was so ugly?

She thought of other women, widowed like herself, and other babies without fathers. Could the desolation of war ever be repaired? Were the hopes and dreams she had known on her walks in the mountains nothing but fantasies? She remembered the words of Keats: ' "Beauty is truth, truth beauty." ' But where was beauty, where was truth?

Prunella was falling asleep. Her eyes opened and closed, the eyelids becoming heavier and heavier each time, until finally they dropped and stayed closed. Mollie rose and leant over the cot. How peaceful her baby looked asleep! A being she and Hugh had created together, untouched by the war, still pure and untarnished.

'I wish Hugh could see her now,' Mollie said, aloud. And then vividly, as though from another world, she had a vision of Hugh in the trenches. She watched him stumbling down the lines, his face bleeding, his left arm hanging at his side. She saw him standing and firing at the advancing enemy; and then falling, as the Germans poured into the trench. It was naked slaughter she saw, war stripped of its glory.

She tried to make sense of it. She could not take refuge in the disciplined rituals which comforted some soldiers' wives. Nor could she cast a gloss over what had happened. Wild, defenceless, she could only suffer. She would continue to suffer, but she would also try to understand.

Prunella stirred in her sleep, then settled again with a small sigh. Mollie adjusted the shawl round the baby's shoulders, and stood upright, her hands at her sides. She closed her eyes.

Slowly the vision of the Himalayas came back to her, each outline, each peak, flooded in rosy light. She stood very still, hardly daring to breathe. And as the moments lengthened, it seemed that Hugh stood beside her, looking with her at the mountains, slipping his hand into her own. For the last time they were together. Then his presence – loving, delicate, ephemeral – withdrew. She was alone.

Her hand rose to her throat. She felt the swelling there – a swelling she had first noticed the morning Hugh had left – felt also the Gurkha brooch he had given her, which was pinned to the collar of her blouse. She remembered its motto, and she whispered, '*I will keep faith.*'

PART TWO

6

'Architects of the Future'

Mollie had stayed in London throughout the war, sharing a flat with her sisters, looking after Prunella and keeping open house for family and friends, many of them soldiers from the Dominions.

She worked each Sunday in a munitions factory, relieving the permanent workers there and taking an interest in their problems and social conditions. As the years passed, these became more acute, for the war demanded the utmost effort and endurance from everyone.

Mollie had suffered her greatest loss at the beginning, when hope for personal happiness had died in her. She held on somehow, gaining a deep fellow-feeling for others who had been bereaved and never losing her loathing for the waste and horror inflicted by war.

When peace came, she longed to do something practical to help other women who had also suffered in the long years of strain. She knew she possessed the means to improve their health and well-being. But how could she put this knowledge to use? She was living on very little money. She had only her army widow's pension and a tiny income of her own. The work she had done for the Conn Institute, and the friends and social life of her Indian years, seemed worlds away.

She kept in touch with Hugh's family, and her sisters gave her companionship, but she realized that the effort needed to return to her profession and make a wider life must come from herself.

I, Prunella, was now four years old. I was an only child, but early in the war my cousin Cinderella had come to live with us. She was the daughter of my mother's brother Harry and was born in India on Christmas Day 1914, six months later than myself. Her mother had died at her birth, her father was on active service in the war, and Mollie offered to look after her. She became part of our family. She and I were brought up like sisters and my mother was mother to her too.

My earliest memories were of the war – searchlights, soldiers and gun emplacements in the park. I and Cinderella – Drella to her family – were taken to play there by our pretty Irish nurse who made friends with the soldiers at the searchlight base. I remember the great glass globe looking like a wide open eye. We wanted to clamber over it, but were stopped; instead we sang songs with the soldiers – 'Tipperary' and 'Pack Up Your Troubles' – and were taught to salute.

We lived in a house in Maida Vale shared with my Aunt Nan; often my other aunts, Norah and Charlie, came to stay. Each summer and Easter we went for holidays to Portrush in Ireland where my grandmother lived. I can remember her house on the headland, the long curve of the sandy beach below, rock-pools with sea-pinks flowering beside them, and the cold, cold sea. Although I dreaded the sea crossing to Ireland, I used to look forward to these holidays each year.

The nicest thing that happened in London was the children's exercise class, which my mother conducted in her drawing-room once a week. Drella and I helped her push back the furniture, roll up the rugs and make a clear space. A pianist arrived to play on our grand piano and the class began. At first there were only four children in it, myself, Drella and Peggy and Joan St Lo. Our mothers were friends and we quickly became close friends too. Drella and I were about five when the class started, Peggy and Joan a few years older.

Every Saturday morning the four of us met, bouncing round the drawing-room in little green tunics, pretending to be flags at half-mast or elephants or bunnies or seals, while my mother adapted her exercises to our needs and imaginations. She trained our bodies to be strong and supple and we grew up knowing her system so well that it became second nature to us. She was funny and vital and loving, but strict also. She had her father's standards of excellence. No fooling around or slacking was allowed. Early on, we learnt to try our hardest.

This children's class opened the way for Mollie to start her work again. It grew and became the nucleus for the large children's classes which later she held at the Mayfair Hotel in Park Lane, and for Violet, Duchess of Rutland, in her private house in Kensington. By 1920 she was teaching small groups of women in her house and running a special evening class for business girls there once a week.

At the same time, she was treating patients sent to her by doctors. One of these was a young boy with chronic asthma whom she decided should come and live with us for three months so that she could supervise his treatment each day. Drella and I objected. We ganged up against the delicate youth, who snorted and sneezed and seemed to be for ever complaining. He disrupted our sway over the household. But we got short shrift from my mother.

'You ought to help him, not criticize him,' she said. 'I rely on you to see that he practises his breathing exercises each morning for at least ten minutes in front of an open window. The sooner he's cured, the sooner he'll leave.'

With this incentive, we co-operated, and in due course the asthma was completely cured.

Another patient was a girl of thirteen suffering from spinal curvature – a severe dorso-lumbar scoliosis – accompanied by extreme thinness, poor appetite and constant colds. The doctor who sent her to Mollie feared that she was incurable. Mollie advised her to leave school and concentrate on getting well.

The pupil wrote:

So for the next four years I went up to Mrs Stack's house at least twice a week for private lessons, and at home practised for anything up to two hours a day. After nearly three years of hard work the lumbar curve had decreased considerably, making me more upright. I could keep my clothes on my left shoulder whereas before they were always slipping off, and Mrs Stack had hopes of making a big impression on the dorsal curve which was by far the worst. My feet were no longer flat. Under her advice I had certain manipulations and some massage treatment and made such marvellous progress that by the time I was seventeen I looked normal.

Cures of this kind required much faith and patience. Mollie was able to inspire in her pupils the enthusiasm necessary for years of painstaking application.

Mrs Conn's system consisted essentially of remedial exercises which aimed to eliminate disabilities by improving posture. The correct positioning of the pelvic region and the training of the spine and abdominal muscles formed its basis, combined with breathing exercises which increased the lung capacity and mobilized the thorax. Mollie now began to develop this system, adding movements of her own; some were influenced by the yoga *asanas* she had studied in India, others invented by herself for graceful deportment and figure training. She also experimented with setting the exercises to music.

'It is impossible to over-estimate the importance of rhythm in body training,' she wrote later.

> Rhythm – moving balance – is Life itself. It exists in the miniature solar system of the atom, with the exact movements of its electrons and protons, as surely as it does in the great solar system itself, with the balanced swing of the planets making music round the sun. It exists in the thrilling waves of sound, in the fast-speeding waves of light; and the more truly we train our bodies in accord with nature's laws, the more we shall set free the body's dormant powers of expressing in itself the rhythm of the universe which welds all nature, and that includes human nature, into one beautiful whole. Rhythm is the secret of personal magnetism.*

For her music, Mollie chose contemporary jazz tunes which could be played on the piano or gramophone and which would add zest to the classes.

By 1923 Mollie felt ready to arrange a lecture-demonstration which she hoped would enlarge the scope of her work. She hired the Aeolian Hall, a concert hall in Wigmore Street, and, through an introduction, approached the King's physician,

---

* Mary Bagot Stack, *Building the Body Beautiful*.

Lord Dawson of Penn, asking him to chair the meeting. She was so convinced of the importance of her work that she was prepared to risk possible rebuff. However, Lord Dawson was impressed by her and agreed to do it.

A large audience assembled and he opened the proceedings, giving her his warm support. Mollie followed with a lecture on her system. Then came the demonstration, supplied by the founder members of her children's class. For weeks, all four of us had been preparing and rehearsing. Joan St Lo, the eldest, was chosen to show the basic health exercises. Drella and I followed, with adaptations for children. And at the end Peggy performed her speciality, a dance called the 'Dragonfly', included to show that exercises could lead to expressive movement.

We had all learnt the dance but Peggy was best at it. Darting round the stage in a shimmering leotard, her arms vibrating like wings, she impressed the audience enormously, especially at the end when she fluttered to the floor with a broken wing and expired, accompanied by a poignant rallentando on the piano.

Mollie's insistence that the 'body of health' which she trained should lead on to the 'body of expression' was in tune with contemporary ideas. In post-war Britain, women were at last free to work, free to vote and free to think for themselves. A different physical ideal was emerging. Isadora Duncan, a pioneer, had freed dance from the limitations of classical ballet and advocated natural movement in bare feet, free from constricting clothing. She was followed by other innovators like Ruby Ginner and Margaret Morris, who were inspired by the art and ideals of ancient Greece. Mollie was working along the same lines and her developing ideas were consolidated by the practical experience gained from training her pupils.

> Little do we realise the delight that awaits us [she wrote] when we have trained the body to be its own instrument within the great orchestra of Life. That orchestra exists as a result of each individual contributing his or her share in harmony with every other. This cannot be done until in each one inner harmony exists, a rhythmic balance of body and spirit. Scientific training of the body along these high

standards was carried out successfully by the Greeks, but then the standards were set by men. Women are the natural race builders of the world. It is they who should be responsible for its physique. In this direction they are the 'Architects of the Future'. Cannot we modern women do as well as the Greeks?*

Mollie longed to put these ideas into practice and to open her own training school on the lines of the Conn Institute. But her institute would go further and include expressive dance, which would balance the remedial exercises with an artistic element. She chose a young teacher, Marjorie Duncombe, from the Ginner-Mawer School of Dance and Drama, to teach her children's class, and a partnership began which was to have undreamt-of results.

Mollie's lecture-demonstration, for which Marjorie produced the dance items, had brought her more pupils and the chance to write articles for the press, but further expansion was frustrated by lack of space and lack of money. In this situation, her sister Nan came to her rescue. She wrote later:

> Mollie was essentially a visionary, and it would have been a tragedy if anything material had ever been allowed to swamp her, or cramp her style. But big ideas are hard to reconcile with a very slender purse, and sometimes it was well nigh impossible to make both ends meet. . . . I felt convinced that if Mollie could get a little more scope, just a tiny chink, she would push open the door to success and forge ahead with her work. If she had a studio where she could give bigger classes, instead of a much too small drawing-room in our house! . . . But how could such a place be found and paid for? All my worldly wealth consisted of a legacy of £250. Still – great schemes have been started before now with less than this. . . . I put my name and my needs on the books of the nearest house-agent.

Two years passed. Difficulties mounted for Mollie, and Nan felt increasingly frustrated. Then suddenly one day the house-agent telephoned her at her office and said, 'I think I have just what you want. A house with an eighty-foot

---

* Mary Bagot Stack, *Building the Body Beautiful*.

drawing-room with a parquet floor, and possibly permission to convert.'

Nan leapt into a taxi, burst in on Mollie, who was having tea at home with Drella and me, and rushed her off to see the house.

'Come quick,' she urged, 'or someone else will take it. The house-agent says there are six people after it.'

Together they entered the drawing-room.

It was a lovely room [Nan wrote] in a regular mansion of a house, with a beautiful garden at the back. I can still see Mollie's radiant expression as she looked around. 'What classes I could hold in a room like this!'

'Mollie, it shall be your studio, *coûte que coûte*,' I said.

'But the risk. The house is so big.'

'No buts, Mollie. We'll convert the top and pay for the whole thing easily.'

'But suppose we get no tenants?'

'Don't suppose, just see them queuing up the stairs.'

The place was heavenly, roses were blooming in our garden (it was already ours) and the sun was setting over the trees in the woods behind. I had a triumphant feeling as I looked out of the drawing-room window and realised that at last I could do something tangible to help. I'd take the house and sign the lease, and then Mollie could forge ahead. She could start her school for teachers, and thus give permanence to her work. She could educate the children, develop her schemes, expand and grow in such surroundings, and not be hampered any longer by lack of space.

£250 was a tiny sum for such a venture, and little did I realise the debt and difficulties I was in for.

Nan went on to describe the entry into the house:

The furniture arrived late in the afternoon and was engulfed in huge, empty spaces. Carpets looked like mats, and curtains like window-blinds in those big, lofty rooms. . . . I was beginning to get cold feet, as I sat waiting for Mollie in the big drawing-room. Why was she so late? I turned on the lights to cheer me up. Would she never come? Why could she not keep an appointment? Suddenly she appeared with a

bottle of champagne under her arm. We were shaking with
excitement. Mollie looked round the room and said, 'My
lovely studio, doesn't it look grand all lit up?'

Her enthusiasm was infectious. At last, at last. Here was
scope; here was happiness. We sat there together in the
middle of that big room. . . . We drank to her schemes, to her
visions of the future.

'*My lovely studio.*' How well we came to know that room! In my
memory it seems always to be flooded with sunlight, enfolded in
music and pervaded by an atmosphere of creative activity. Its
large sash windows gave on to the garden; one wall had mirrors
and a dance-barre running down the length of it; a grand piano
stood in one corner; otherwise it was empty except for yards of
space waiting to be filled above that beautiful parquet floor.

The house was in Holland Park, a quiet residential district of
London. Its garden bordered the Ilchester Estate whose woods
stretched for a mile or so to Kensington High Street. Birds flew
in from the trees and sang in the garden. There was a country
atmosphere, undisturbed by noise of the busy city outside.
Mollie could not have wished for a more ideal setting.

We moved into this house in 1925. Nan took responsibility
for converting the top floors into apartments and letting them,
while Mollie set about collecting students for the opening of her
training school.

Build the Body Beautiful
at the Bagot Stack Health School.

This was the grandiose title she chose for her embossed letter
headings. It was accompanied by two photographs and a list of
the subjects taught. The cable address in the top right-hand
corner proclaimed *Bodybild, London.* Mollie had started as she
meant to go on!

Dance would form an important part of her curriculum. But
what type of dance? It must be free and spontaneous, closely
linked to nature and natural expression, and based on the same
principles as her own training for the body of health. Mollie
found all these qualities in the Revived Greek Dance of Ruby

Ginner, based on the forms of movement illustrated on ancient Greek pottery, painting and sculpture, already familiar to Mollie from her training with Mrs Conn.

Ruby Ginner was a pioneer like herself, who had founded her training school in 1914 and gone on to form a Greek Dance Association and hold examinations with the Royal Academy of Dancing. Her work was later widely taught in schools and colleges and influenced the generations that grew up in the 1920s and 1930s, forming a basis for the modern dance to which many afterwards graduated. The Greek dance technique was expressive and natural, and movement was closely related to the music. The dancing, often improvised, could be lyrical, soft and fluid, or athletic, strong and dramatic.

Marjorie Duncombe, chosen by Mollie, taught Greek dance to her children's class. We all loved it and much admired Marjorie. We learnt nature rhythms, pretending to be flowers opening, butterflies fluttering round the room, trees tossing in the wind or waves breaking on the shore. We had sessions of improvisation, when we would listen to a piece of classical music and then move to it, each interpreting it in her own way. We studied the Greek friezes: eight arm positions were taken from classical vases and adapted for basic body training. And, best of all, we indulged in the Greek tragedies, which involved beating our breasts, tearing our hair and banging our clenched fists one against the other in dramatic despair.

For these purposes we wore Greek tunics of a classical style, set off by a severe headband across our foreheads. We also learnt dances like the 'Dragonfly'. Marjorie entered us for a public competition in which each of us gained a prize for a solo dance, and the group carried off a cup.

My mother was delighted by this success but she did not allow us to become complacent. She was always determined that we should reach a high standard. She had a sharp eye for detail and was meticulous in preparation, rehearsing us until we were 'foolproof', as she called it. Sometimes we rebelled. A few early photographs of me show a sulky child posing unwillingly in the required position. But by and large we wanted to please her. Her praise was not given easily and was considered worth having.

Her capacity for affection and interest in others now

increasingly went into her work. She was 'Mummy' to all four
of us children (Peggy and Joan called her 'Mummy No. 2').
Marjorie also became a great friend. She wrote later: 'Mollie's
ideas of training the body coincided so exactly with mine. And
her abundance of humour was always ready to bubble up on
the slightest provocation.'

By September 1925 ten students had been collected for the
training school. Marjorie became Mollie's partner and
together they drew up a syllabus. During her three-year
training at the Ginner-Mawer School of Dance and Drama,
Marjorie had studied Greek dancing, ballet, national dancing,
composition, mime and voice production. She now taught all
these subjects at the Bagot Stack Health School, while Mollie
dealt with the health exercises (practical and remedial),
ballroom dancing and public speaking. A visiting doctor was
the tutor for anatomy and physiology.

It was an ambitious programme. But several of the first set of
students were already experienced in Mollie's and Marjorie's
classes, and Peggy and Joan St Lo, now old enough to train,
had practised the exercises from childhood. Mollie's young
spinal patient also joined the course, now that her cure was
complete.

Ten nervous girls assembled in the bare studio on the first
day of term. They listened to an introductory talk by Mollie,
followed by an exhilarating class. Anatomy and physiology
instruction was hard work, but they recovered during
Marjorie's strenuous dance sessions and went home tired but
enthusiastic. Marjorie later described what happened next:

All went swimmingly until about the third week, when the
school very nearly came to an untimely end. . . . It happened
one afternoon when I was taking a class of Voice Production
and all of us were being very serious and the girls rather
nervous and shy. Suddenly the door opened and in walked
Mollie's sister Nan, dressed in the very abbreviated costume
of an artiste of the *Folies Bergère*. She thought it a terrific joke
and was dumbfounded at my expression of extreme
horror. . . . Finishing the lesson abruptly, I hurried away to
tell Mollie. To this day I shall never forget her expression as I
related the dire news. 'Marjorie,' she wailed, between tears

and laughter, 'this is the end of our school.' For days we waited in fear and trembling for letters from irate parents asking us exactly what kind of a training we were giving their daughters.

Nan was unrepentant. She had recently taken up dress designing and had just invented a very revealing cabaret costume. She could not resist showing it off to the nearest audience, and failed to see why the appearance of a nearly naked woman should jeopardize the success of Mollie's school, a project very close to her heart.

Early in the following year, 1926, Mollie's mother died. She had been living in Portrush since 1915, where we had visited her regularly. Her death was sudden and unexpected. She was only seventy-four.

Mollie and Nan travelled to Ireland for the funeral, which was held in a little church at Cappagh, near Omagh, where Charlotte had grown up. Standing among the family graves, Mollie may have thought of the holiday at Mullaghmore when her mother had nursed her back to health; of her support during the time of the divorce; of their time together in Manchester; of the comfort she had given her when the dreadful news came of the circumstances of Hugh's death.

Mollie, a parent herself now, watched her mother's coffin being lowered to lie beside her father in the next grave. Later she wrote to Norah, now married and living in India: 'I looked at Mother and I knew strongly that her body was no more than an old discarded garment, its part played; and I felt her real self near me, that she was going to help me. . . . I am sure that soon we and others will pierce the veil of this mystery and death (as we know it) will be conquered.'

Mollie's 'lovely studio' was now in constant use. The students trained there all day and Mollie held evening classes several times a week. She also used it for gatherings of her friends. Irene Scharrer, the famous concert pianist, lived across the road and would drop in to play on the grand piano. Drella and I would be prevailed on to dance to entertain Mollie's guests. And often, before the end of the evening, the guests themselves would act in one of the charades which Mollie loved to organize; Marjorie described her 'tucking her evening dress into her pants and posing, with a roguish smile on her face and an apple on her head, as William Tell'.

By the autumn the students had completed the first year of their training. Their next major challenge was a charity matinée, in aid of the City of London Maternity Hospital, at the Comedy Theatre. This performance took place on 17 November 1926. The programme was divided into two sections: 'Health', which consisted of a talk by Mollie and a demonstration of her exercises; and 'Grace and Expression', in which dance items arranged and produced by Marjorie Duncombe were presented.

Weeks of rehearsal went into this show, for which we were taught to use stage make-up, including wet-white lotion for our bare arms and legs, and stage lighting. Marjorie, Peggy and Joan danced a number in which they represented golden statuettes come to life; they wore long net skirts bordered with sequins over gold leotards and had gold balls attached to their wrists. Drella and I performed with six other children in 'The Dancing Lesson', our ages ranging from four to twelve. I was the eldest. I also took the leading part in an item called 'Philippa the Fair'. I had written a medieval ballad which began:

> The sweetest girl on all the earth
> Was Philippa the Fair.
> Her eyes were blue and full of mirth
> And golden was her hair.

It went on in this vein for a number of stanzas and Nan had set it to music. Mollie, with her unerring instinct for publicity, realized the publicity value of an 'authoress-actress of twelve years old'. So the ballad was staged, with myself in medieval dress as Philippa, and one of the students as the troubadour serenading me beneath a window. Sure enough, pictures appeared in most of the leading papers.

After the show, Violet, Duchess of Rutland, whose

1 Hugh Stack, father of Prunella

2 Mollie Stack, aged three (*left*) with her sister Nan, aged four and a half

3 Mollie Stack in 1932

4 Prunella, aged thirteen

5 Peggy St Lo's famous leap,
chosen as the League's
emblem.

committee had invited Mollie to produce the programme, wrote: 'We were quite enchanted with the performance yesterday afternoon. . . . My little grand-daughter says she wants lessons from Mrs Bagot Stack. . . . I thought all the dancing was lovely.'

In the summer of 1927 the first training course ended and the newly qualified teachers started classes of their own. Peggy and Joan joined the cast of a musical comedy called *Lucky Girl*, which ran at the London Pavilion Theatre for eighteen months and then went on tour. Before long, Peggy was appointed ballet mistress to the chorus, a remarkable feat for a girl of seventeen and a tribute to her previous training. She and Joan developed their stage presence and learnt tap-dancing; they brought these skills back to Mollie's school when they returned after a year or so to work for her.

Meantime, I had joined the second training course. Drella and I had attended Norland Place School, a day-school nearby which we enjoyed. But I was now thirteen and needed a change of scene. I was already deeply involved in my mother's work. I frequently posed for photographs and was upheld as an example of the benefits of her training in her many articles for the press. She decided that my academic lessons should continue with a tutor – an Oxford graduate friend of hers – and I should attend full-time as a student of the Bagot Stack Health School. The first course had proved its value and she had no qualms about committing me to the second one. So Drella and I were separated. She went off to boarding-school and in September 1927 I started my new training.

I never regretted my mother's decision. Her graduate friend broadened my interests, and the dance training taught me self-discipline, provided me with an outlet for self-expression, and its high standards gave me a yardstick by which to measure other achievements. It was, of course, a confined world. But everyone in it worked very hard and felt committed to Mollie's ideals. And, for me, there were always new challenges to be met – a dance to be learnt, a performance to be rehearsed, an essay to be completed.

My relationship with my mother had a public and private

aspect. In public, she expected unqualified co-operation, even if I sometimes rebelled against being starred as 'the perfect girl'. In private, she was wonderfully loving and tender. Because there was no Hugh, we each felt responsible for the other, and tried to make up to one another for his absence. Although I had never known my father, Mollie made him live for me; he set a standard of courage, honesty and integrity for me to try to achieve. And of course Mollie was great fun to be with; always spontaneous, humorous and original.

Like most pioneers, Mollie reflected the spirit of her age but had the vision to see further. She was too involved in her own technique and ideas to have much contact with others in her field, but in fact in the 1920s foundations were being laid for several important later developments. The training schools of Margaret Morris and Ruby Ginner were already well established, having opened in 1910 and 1914, and in 1920 the Association of Operatic Dancing was formed. This represented the four main schools of classical ballet training then recognized in Europe – Italian, French, Danish and Russian. It inaugurated professional examinations for teachers and dancers and in 1935 became the Royal Academy of Dancing.

At the same time, Marie Rambert, in 1920, and Ninette de Valois, in 1926, were opening schools linked to their dance companies. These produced exceptional dancers and choreographers and became famous the world over as the Ballet Rambert and the Vic-Wells, later the Royal Ballet.

Such schools developed professional standards of performance – standards the average girl or woman could not hope to attain. But their example generated an interest in dance and a desire to participate. Mollie, too, was training professionals in her school; but she was also much concerned with the needs of working girls and women, the sort of people who could not afford an expensive course and had not the talent to become professional dancers but who nevertheless wanted to train their bodies and enjoy movement. She had classes for them in the evenings in her studio, or at the shops and City offices where they worked; and she found in these pupils an enthusiasm that made her long to help them more.

By 1930 her work had progressed remarkably. Her students had given two more charity performances. One was at the

Norwich Hippodrome in aid of the Bishop of Norwich's Fund
for Church Schools, where Marjorie produced some striking
items, including a Greek pyrrhic dance for which we wore
tunics and headbands and wielded bows and arrows, swords,
shields and spears – all painted white – with expressions of
suitable ferocity. (This was my favourite dance!) And another
at a Snow Ball at Claridge's Hotel in London, in aid of the City
of London Maternity Hospital. Among other items, Peggy took
time off from her stage career to dance the 'Dragonfly' once
more.

Summer holidays were spent at Dinard or St Malo in
Brittany, where Mollie and Marjorie ran a summer school for
their students and friends, and we exercised and danced on the
sands. Marjorie wrote of this time: 'Mollie on holiday was an
ideal companion, so unselfish and sporting, ready to bathe on
the coldest of days and to play tennis with the worst of players.
She herself excelled in tennis and golf and many helpful hints
she gave me concerning my own game.' She also kept her eye on
the ball with regard to publicity, and arranged to have a series
of attractive photographs taken with which she flooded the
press when we returned to England.

My training ended in the summer of 1930 when I was sixteen. I
had been at the Bagot Stack Health School for three years and
was now a qualified teacher with an honours certificate. I had
gained greatly from the training. Marjorie possessed the ability
to draw the maximum out of her students, and she instilled in
me a love of music and movement which has lasted to this day.
Mollie taught me to concentrate, to insist on high standards,
and to present my work with humour. But I was too young to
teach. Also some aspects of my academic lessons had suffered;
except for anatomy and physiology, science subjects had been
almost entirely neglected.

It was decided that I should go to a boarding-school for a
year, in spite of the fact that my mother much needed my help.
Exciting new developments were taking place. Nevertheless,
unselfishly she let me go. I told her I wanted a change; I wished
to lead an ordinary life, free from publicity, and to gain
experience of being an average girl living with girls of her own

age. The predictable routine a traditional education seemed quite glamorous to me!

So in September 1930 I set off, leaving behind my tunics, leotards, tights and ballet shoes, and taking with me a large tin trunk full of hideous school clothes. And Mollie bravely shrugged off feelings of loneliness, got up at 6.30 a.m. each day and completed her book, *Building the Body Beautiful*, on which she had been engaged.

7

Movement Is Life

For the last year Mollie had been setting down her system of exercises. In the introduction to her book she took her readers into her confidence, writing in a personal, vivid style which formed a close contact between them and herself.

It is easy to sit and dream ideals, but 'action is the prayer that is answered' and to the visionary this is a particularly hard lesson to learn. Still, to those of us who force ourselves into harness, action brings its own reward in widened horizon, clearer vision and mental muscle. . . . The glorious edifice exists in the mind of the builder before he begins, but stone by stone it has to be constructed, and the monotonous placing of the stones of life is the thing which human nature usually shies at – and so fails. One of the secrets of achievement is to find means of making the 'placing of the stones' as enjoyable and effortless as possible.

The Body Beautiful, which is the aim of our building, forms no exception to these rules. We all have our visions of our bodies as we would like them to be, if we are to lead our fullest, best and happiest lives, but to get down to action and make them so, is another matter. . . .

Reader, even now my pen is flagging at the effort this book is costing me; being Irish and a dreamer, I have learned very hardly the value of daily disciplined action; so my heart goes out to other weaklings, like myself, who yawn and say, 'Oh dear, must I begin?'

Yes, you must. Certainly, give your imagination free play,

but let those filmy dreams of yours take definite shape. . . .

Imagination plus *enthusiastic action*. . . . What force on earth can withstand these two combined?

Mollie then went on to describe exercises for the spine, the abdomen, the feet, ankles and knees, the hips and legs, the waist, the shoulders, arms and hands, and the circulation. In addition, there were sections on breathing and skin airing, common ailments and diet, graceful walking, and grace and balance. The exercises were graduated from easy to advanced in a training sequence that would take ten weeks. Mollie illustrated her text with photographs of her students and lightened it with touches of humour. She maintained a personal touch throughout and ended with these words:

> Now, dear reader – and you are dear, for have we not been working together intimately and constructively for ten weeks – if this book turns out to be of the slightest value to you, please have mercy and forgive its shortcomings.
>
> I quoted at the beginning the words 'action is the prayer that is answered'. This bit of action is now over for me, *thank Heaven*. I am rather glad I can return to sitting with my heels on the mantelpiece, and in my heart a glorious vision of a world where the women are so beautiful that they are an inspiration, not a temptation, for thus the happy future of the whole human race will be assured.

Building the Body Beautiful appeared in May 1931 and went through a number of subsequent editions.

The *Sunday Referee* declared the book 'admirably adapted to the needs of, let us say, the ordinary young woman who must work for her living and who can only utilise her leisure in health-giving and beautifying exercises. . . . An indispensable volume to be read, marked and learned by women of all ages.' And in fact the young working woman was exactly the type of reader for whom Mollie had written. For in the last year a great new development had taken place. She had founded the Women's League of Health and Beauty.

For a long time she had held classes for business girls, office workers and shop employees and found them among the most appreciative and rewarding of her pupils. These girls worked long hours, earned low salaries and had little opportunity during their scanty leisure time to indulge in dance or sport. Mollie had a strong desire to do something for them: to make more classes available at a price which they could afford; to organize them somehow into a movement which would put her ideal of health training into practice. But where was she to start? Describing her initial inspiration she later wrote:

These intangible, vague dreams had to be translated into practical action. I set my hard-faced friend – my alarm clock – to 6.45 a.m. When it rang with that slap on the brain which sends all day and night dreams flying, I jumped out of bed, said my prayers, had a cold bath, opened my windows, stripped off my clothes and set going on my gramophone the gayest jazz tune I could find, and I exercised around my bedroom, in physical bliss but mental blankness.

Suddenly, in the middle of these bodily activities, I found I was thinking – thinking hard. My brain (such as it was, and, unfortunately, still is) was beginning to work. Ideas came, and came, and more ideas came, until at last they were pouring in so fast I could not catch them. Some mental tap had been unloosed from somewhere – from where, who knows?

Mental inertia was going, mental alertness was coming. I opened my windows wider, I breathed deeper. Laziness – mental and physical – (the root of most failure) was going – and then – and then – the Idea came. If Energy is the source of life, and if we women want – as we all do – Life, *we must have energy*.

How? – a league – a League of Women who will renew their energy in themselves and for themselves day by day. A League of Women pledged (so as to keep us lazy things at it) to breathe, to leap – and, above all, to think. . . .

Furiously I picked up a pencil and made notes of how to begin – how to go on. . . . I can feel now the tumbling excitement, the fury, the fun of the first great push, i.e., getting the League down on paper. . . . I did not then foresee the misery of getting it off the paper again. The anxieties, the

crowding responsibilities, the indecisions and decisions.
Those came later.

I only saw before my eyes, in letters of flame, 'The
Women's League.' League of what? League of Energy? No,
that would be too terrifying to the lazy, a frontal attack,
always dangerous. League of Health? But no, that was
utterly dull; it had none of the sparkle most women love –
sparkling necklaces, bangles, rings, and eyes – sparkling
thoughts, too, surely!

Then floated into my mind – 'build-the-body-beautiful' –
the title of the book that I had just begun to write: A
Build-the-Body-Beautiful-League? – I see now how unsuitable was the title. But the big 'B' for Beauty – the ideal
Beauty which I was writing about in my book attracted me,
and so eventually our first endeavours started under that
clumsy title!

My heart sang all the day. . . . But in the middle of that
night I awoke with a start from a financial nightmare.
Warfare was afoot, a very subtle form of warfare. The
belligerents were Rent v. Health. In the dark I lay and
thought anxiously. If I dropped my private school and went
into the arena of life to form a huge League, how could it be
financed?

The source of my finances lay chiefly in my school: my
daughter had to be educated – my rents had to be paid –
my-my-my – I-I-I – I was already forging my own chains,
putting the brake on my own endeavour.

Then my thoughts grew hazy, my anxious head cuddled
down on the pillow, my dreams came back . . . and in the
night, believe me or not, as you choose, I heard a voice
saying, 'Back the League.'

The next few months saw a spectacular success. Mollie hired a
large hall in central London, transferred her evening classes
there and charged only sixpence each so that her classes would
be available to everyone. She provided expert teachers from
the first batch of students, now fully trained, and they found
themselves coping with classes of seventy or eighty women and
girls as new members poured in. It cost 2s. 6d. to join the

League and 2s. for an entrance badge, to be worn at every class. The emblem chosen for the badge was the leaping figure of Peggy St Lo, with the motto *Movement Is Life* inscribed beneath. For exercising, the members wore an up-to-date version of Mrs Conn's uniform: white blouses and black satin pants, which grew shorter and shorter as the years passed.

Mollie had struck a chord which evoked an instant response. People were enthusiastic about joining associations at that time, and the word League was in vogue. There was a League of Nations, an Overseas League and a League of Health and Strength (for men).

Mollie's League started in March 1930 and within three months it was one thousand strong. It had started with £16, subscribed by the sixteen founder members. Most people would have sought sponsorship or financial aid, but Mollie was convinced that the League could be self-supporting if enough members joined it.

During this initial period of the League's development I was still training at the Bagot Stack Health School, preparing to go to boarding-school in September, and I became involved in Mollie's next step. Publicity, she felt, was essential. For the League to be financially viable, she must recruit members rapidly. But how was she to achieve this without a large outlay in advertising? Again, the answer came to her during her early morning exercising: she would organize a public display in Hyde Park to the music of a military band!

With her customary audacity, she called on the Right Honourable George Lansbury, a well-known socialist, then First Commissioner of Works, in charge of public places.

She wrote:

Outside his door my knees knocked together, but under my arm I carried what, to me, was an open sesame – pictures of the vast Sokol movement in Czecho-Slovakia, fourteen thousand people exercising together in perfect unity and perfect formation. My brain was throbbing to the phrases *'Movement is Life'* – *'Eight members are potentially eight million'* –

'*Health for Everyone*' – and then the door opened, and, instead of a fiercely businesslike official, I saw a fatherly, rosy-cheeked, old gentleman. . . .

For five minutes I poured on him (quite unnecessarily) a Niagara of persuasion. He emerged from it smiling, and said, 'Of course you can have Hyde Park – Hyde Park is for the people.'

Mollie expected a thousand members to march into Hyde Park that Saturday. In fact only 150 came. But they made history. Nothing like this had ever taken place before. A Mr Hay, Superintendent of Hyde Park, told Mollie so. She apologized for giving him trouble.

'That's all right, Mrs Stack,' he said. 'We're used to all kinds of cranks here.'

But when the members marched forward through the trees to the band of the Queen Victoria's Rifles, the Serpentine behind them and a faint breeze stirring the gaily coloured flags, a sudden cheer burst from the crowd. Some of them were families and friends of the girls demonstrating, but most of them consisted of people who happened to be in the park that afternoon – women with prams and children, men with dogs, young couples out for a walk – people who had stopped to watch out of curiosity, but stayed to admire.

Peggy St Lo and I led the members in, accompanied by the teachers and students of the Bagot Stack Health School. The school had opened less than five years before but had now become the spearhead of a movement that was to attract over a hundred thousand women.

George Lansbury wrote to Mollie that evening, 'This brings a thousand congratulations. It was just splendid; the girls looked healthy and beautiful. I am very glad my Department gave you a chance. If you want to give another show, later on, ask. Best wishes.'

The Hyde Park display had achieved exactly what my mother hoped for – widespread public interest in her work. Every post brought press cuttings from all over Britain, as well as from India, Australia, New Zealand and South Africa. But she was not yet equipped to deal with this demand. The League had only a small number of teachers available to open new centres. It possessed no capital to finance expansion. It depended entirely on its members for its income. And now, during the summer months of July and August, that income dropped alarmingly. Members went on holiday; they swam and played tennis. No one wanted to exercise indoors during the height of the summer. Money dwindled.

Mollie suffered an acute attack of what she called polar feet. Had she been rash? She realized her lack of foresight and experience in undertaking this great project.

Also she was not well. The swelling which had appeared the day after Hugh departed for the war and which she now knew was due to an enlarged thyroid gland had lately increased alarmingly. She consulted a specialist who said that the growth must be removed. So in July 1930 she underwent an operation. From the hospital she wrote to me:

I have your smiling picture here and it lights up the whole room. . . . When you get this I shall be about all right and sleeping peacefully, so I hope you will have been spared any unnecessary anxiety which is bad for small daughters. And now comes the jolly part – a beautiful tidy shapely neck in a few weeks' time and fitness to appear on the subject of Health in Hyde Park next summer without feeling self-conscious about my neck.

Unfortunately, the operation was not entirely successful. The specialist told my mother that the thyroid gland had burst its capsule and it had not been possible to remove all the enlarged growth. Without an operation she would have died. He now hoped for a complete recovery, but if the swelling returned within two years her condition would become serious.

Hiding her disappointment, Mollie made light of this diagnosis, and we went for a holiday to Donegal in Ireland where we stayed with her sister Norah, now married to Major A.J. Cruickshank of the Royal Engineers and home on leave from India.

As before, the landscape of Ireland brought Mollie new vitality. Her energy and enthusiasm returned. By the time we returned to London she was sure of her next step: expansion to the provinces. A cousin had written to her offering to organize

the opening of a League centre in Belfast. The ideal teacher was
at hand – Eileen MacMurray, an Irish girl and one of
Mollie's first students at the Bagot Stack Health School. There
would just be time to conduct the opening meeting before I
departed for my boarding-school. So in the autumn of 1930 we
travelled back to Ireland, this time to Belfast.

The press took pictures of Eileen and myself which appeared
in all the papers. This attracted a crowd to the preliminary
afternoon meeting on the opening day. After speaking, Mollie
invited all those attending to return again in the evening and
bring their friends to the big lecture-demonstration that would
launch the League. And they came, bringing their own friends
and everybody else's friends. The hall was packed. The
meeting went marvellously, and when Mollie offered to teach a
class there and then, enthusiastic women from all over the hall
elbowed their way on to the floor to take part. Practically the
whole audience either joined the League on the spot or took
away forms to fill in and bring along to the first class.

Imagine what it was like for me, adjusting from all this to the
claustrophobic world of a girls' school! At times I had rebelled
against being thrust into the limelight, resented the time spent
in preparations for photographs and wished for a conventional
upbringing and a conventional mother. Now my desire for an
ordered life was fulfilled with a vengeance and I found myself
having to adjust to a world utterly different from hers. I felt
lonely and lost. I had little in common with the other girls and
resented the narrow school discipline. But I did learn some
useful lessons: how to endure team games; how to enjoy the
English countryside; how to appreciate English literature; how
to live in a community; and how, if necessary, to disguise my
feelings. In short, I grew up.

For the next year I was at one remove from the League's
development. However, in May 1931 my headmistress allowed
me weekend leave to attend the second Hyde Park show and the
first display in the Royal Albert Hall. Five hundred members
took part, including a wildly enthusiastic contingent from
Belfast, who at the end of the performance carried their teacher
Eileen MacMurray on their shoulders right up the broad front

staircase of the Albert Hall and into the Royal Box.

My mother kept in touch with affectionate letters, some of which contained exhortations similar to those she had received as a schoolgirl from her father.

She wrote:

> On the whole I am satisfied with your character up to the present. The main things are right – loyalty, generosity, pluck, truth, artistic taste in everything and insight, *a great deal*. The application of these to everyday mundane affairs is the thing.
>
> By the summer you'll have learned a lot. What you need now is concentration. I advise you to analyse every day at every lesson how much you concentrated during each minute, and you'll find long patches of dreamland where you were not listening at all. Eliminate these until you go to practise your exercises and dance and then let them loose and have your fill of dreamland for half an hour each day.

But half an hour was not nearly enough! I found it impossible to limit my dreams to a scheduled time. For now they were full not only of the romance typical of my age, but also of the exciting League events my mother described. By the time I left school in July 1931 I was counting the days until I could resume my work with her.

'Prunella, I need you very badly,' she had written in one of her last letters. And when we were together again I realized why. She had just taken a momentous and very courageous decision.

After the Albert Hall show members poured in and the classes became so crowded that it was imperative to find new and larger halls. As her sister Nan had done six years earlier, Mollie told a house-agent that she wanted permanent premises suitable for headquarters in central London.

A week later she was standing inside a large building called the Mortimer Halls in Great Portland Street, near Oxford Circus. How many of the League's early teachers and members remember that place! It had a big shop window and two spacious halls, one on the ground floor, one in the basement, as well as cloakroom and office accommodation. The halls were former auction rooms, dusty, dirty and uncared for, but Mollie's imagination filled them with active, enthusiastic women. She paced up and down the empty rooms trying to do her calculations.

The rent was £1,500 a year, rising to £2,000. There was £180 in the League's bank account. If she added the small surplus in her own bank she would have enough money to pay the first quarter's rent. The League's membership was two thousand. If each member attended one class a week over forty weeks of the year, the rent would be covered. If they each brought in two new members the turnover would be doubled.

That almighty IF [she wrote]. What a short but powerful word! It represents life as it is, one vast uncertainty, full of tremendous risk. 'IF', at first, became a nightmare of fear to me, but I have learned now how to twist its tail. It is quite simple. When faith comes in, IF goes out. Faith in the importance of your work, your destiny, call it what you will. It seems to me now useless to work at all, unless your work, however insignificant, has this quality of faith. 'Do the thing and the power comes.' I believe it. The great difficulty is to choose the right work and be *sure*. Indecision wrecks many lives and enterprises. Decision comes from wise thinking and wisdom depends on instinctive feeling. . . . Once having thought slowly and wisely, the solution will float into the mind 'instinctively'. When it does, we should act quickly while our enthusiasm is at its height and never look back but always forward.

I thought, and at last I knew, we must take the Mortimer Halls, whether we were really financially safe or not.

In that summer of 1931, the nation, too, was going through a financial crisis. After the New York stock market crash in 1929, it was experiencing the worst slump ever known. Unemployment figures increased each day and a run on the pound threatened the City of London as a world banking and financial centre. Ramsay Macdonald, the Labour Prime Minister, sought the co-operation of the Conservative and Liberal leaders and in August 1931 a National Government was formed.

Soon after, Mollie wrote to her members, 'As salaries are down, and prices cut, and the future is in some people's estimation hazardous, it is more than ever necessary for us women to stand together, and prove that all is well, business is as usual, and we fear nothing.' She went on to tell them of the opportunity presented by the Mortimer Halls premises and her decision to lease them. She asked for their co-operation in increased attendance at class and a drive for new members. And she ended her letter:

> Had I not faith in the ideals of our League and the loyalty of our members to each other the responsibility for one person would be too heavy; but shared by two thousand now and two million potential members, it has no terrors for me. . . . Let us hold on to our ideal of Health, and as before, continue in sympathetic co-operation with one another, and there can be no risk attaching to this forward step.

Six hundred members came to the opening of the Mortimer Halls on 4 November. They sat on the floor, because there were no chairs, and listened attentively to speeches from Mollie, Peggy St Lo and myself. Mollie's letter had moved them. They identified with her ideals and believed, like her, that women who banded together could be a constructive force for peace. Mollie had an exhilarating evening with her 'dear grass roots' before financial worries once more demanded her attention and 'unforeseen sundries' swiftly swallowed up her meagre budget.

Peggy and I ran the office by day and taught classes every night of the week. Members flocked into them. Peggy's stage experience added glamour and she and Joan, who soon joined her, introduced tap-dancing to the League's range of classes and produced cabaret items for the big shows. Mollie was buoyant and optimistic, the members immensely enthusiastic, and the whole Mortimer Halls venture seemed to me certain to succeed. Little did I realize on what a knife-edge success or failure was balanced. For in the spring of 1932 the swelling in Mollie's neck had begun to return.

That year saw a third Hyde Park demonstration, another

display in the Albert Hall and a march down Oxford Street to the music of a military band. Members wore their new outdoor uniform designed by Nan – short black velvet skirts and capes – and onlookers viewed them with amused indulgence.

In August, my mother sent me down to Bournemouth to conduct classes on the beach with Joan St Lo. We demonstrated our exercise routines on a small platform erected on the sand and were accompanied by a three-piece jazz band. Then we held an open class for all the spectators – men, women and children – and handed out leaflets and League magazines. This aroused much interest in visitors from other parts of Britain. In the autumn, new centres opened in Birmingham and Glasgow, as well as around London, and by the end of 1932 total membership had increased to 4,500 members.

At this period Mollie *was* the League. It depended almost entirely on her – her vision, her financial commitment and her inspiration. We young teachers helped, and Marjorie Duncombe continued to exert her unique artistic influence at the Bagot Stack Health School, producing imaginative items for the national displays. But for the League's continued growth and success Mollie's presence was vital.

Early in 1933 this was dangerously threatened. Mollie realized that she could no longer ignore the swelling in her throat. She consulted her specialist who told her that an immediate operation was imperative. He could not guarantee permanent recovery, but without it she would live only for six months. The growth in her neck had become malignant.

Mollie went home to consider her options. She wrote to her sister Norah:

> I have forty people directly depending on my efforts. I believe, in some queer way, the country is depending on them too. I believe, if I desert the League now, it will go under. *I cannot desert it.* Besides, I feel so completely well. . . . the doctors may be wrong. . . . I think we will choose the constructive way of prayer and faith and work. . . . You know how I loathe operations.

6 Prunella, aged twenty, after taking over leadership of the League.

7 David Douglas-Hamilton and Prunella at the time of their engagement

8 Prunella with her eldest son Diarmaid in 1940

9 Scottish members of the League performing an advanced exercise sequence at the Royal Albert Hall.

10 A League teacher (*left*) and a member in a dance pose, 1987

She told me of her decision, not minimizing the seriousness of the diagnosis but stressing the power of the body to heal itself and the power of prayer. She firmly believed in both. Together we put them into practice. She continued teaching her classes, and we went each Sunday to the communion service at All Souls' Church, Langham Place, near the Mortimer Halls, where we prayed for her health. And she seemed radiantly well. To us it was like a miracle. As the months and then years passed I was in danger of taking her recovery for granted. But I think she always knew the price that might have to be paid.

During that year League membership reached 30,000. Mollie devised a new way of keeping in touch with her members. She launched a magazine called *Mother and Daughter* which served as a link between the centres and contained news and views, attractive illustrations and articles of general interest. Mollie consulted Norah, now an experienced journalist, about contents and format, and the following year Norah became Editor, gaining a valuable insight into the workings of the League. By then membership had doubled to 60,000. Fifty students were in training at the Bagot Stack Health School, which had moved from Holland Park to the Mortimer Halls, and a number of new centres were scheduled to open in the autumn.

Mollie's work had captured the imagination of a generation of women. In spite of the League's size, she maintained a personal touch. Her young teachers were trained to value the individuality of their members. In class, everyone was on first name terms and everyone wore the same exercise kit, so that differences of class or background disappeared. Above all, the sessions were fun. The lively contemporary music, the enthusiastic young teachers and the presence of so many others made body training enjoyable. And Mollie's idealism, her rejection of the commercial, and her belief in her work permeated to every centre, even the smallest and most remote.

In May 1934 the national displays were preceded by a service at All Souls' Church, where many members assembled to give thanks and renew their fellowship. This was followed by a march down Oxford Street and a performance in Hyde Park of 1,000 members. Then came the Albert Hall displays, on two successive evenings.

By now members were used to the maze of underground entrances from which they had to flood into the arena. They entered in their hundreds, while others marched over the platform and down the aisle stairways, carrying banners proclaiming the cities and countries from which they had come, the Scots with tartan shoulders ribbons, the Irish with green. Here was a mass gathering to demonstrate the fellowship of women, united to realize an ideal in which Mollie had made them believe.

Standing on the platform like a flame in her long red dress she spoke to them all.

Life has taught me many things, and above all a deep sense of comradeship with humanity. It was this growing sense of comradeship, I suppose, which first gave me the idea of this League. . . . Because I see a goal further ahead than Health and Beauty, in the ordinary sense, and that is Peace, and further on stands Love – Universal Love and Service. Human health and beauty are but the stepping-stones to that ideal. . . . Health represents peace and harmonious balance in the innermost tissues of mind and body. Beauty seems to me to represent this idea carried out by every individual, by humanity universally. . . . Peace must finally come to the world by our own determination to make it come. Each individual counts.

The last item of the show expressed this ideal most effectively. She described it later in a letter to Norah:

The biggest success, I think, was the finale. Prunella and I produced it together. It started with a representation of the last war. First a bugle blew faintly and with dim lights a slow trail of girls came in, their heads and hands hanging, some bandaged, one carrying a 'wounded' man on her back, one blind. . . . They formed a line below the platform to the music of the 'Long, Long Trail' and 'Tipperary'. Then the bugle called louder and the faint singing of 'Marching Feet', the League song, was heard outside the scenes. The light grew stronger and hundreds of girls in uniform streamed and streamed in singing. . . . it was really a great moment. Then from the opposite staircase, the tallest girls and teachers carried triumphantly a long cloth of gold which they spread right down the arena and up to the platform steps. There was a jangle and clash – Capital and Labour, Marjorie and Peggy, clattered up the golden path, until they reached the steps, when the faint sound of melodious music crept out and they and all the other heads slowly turned towards the opposite staircase, down which slowly and marvellously came Prunella in gold with gold wings trailing. It took two or three minutes for her to reach the platform steps, yet everyone sat still, riveted by the music and the idea. Slowly Capital dropped his cloak and Labour her rags and appeared, as they are, equal in silver. Peace lifted them as she passed up the steps and joined their hands – it was faultless and most people were so moved they could not help weeping. We had taken a chance and succeeded in putting over the idea of *Peace*.

By late June Mollie had taken care of most of her pressing commitments. She had just completed a set of gramophone records demonstrating her system and was about to embark on the students' summer examinations.

On the first Sunday in July we drove out of London for a picnic in the country with some friends. Nan was there and so was Drella who was staying with us. We sat and talked in the brilliant summer sunshine. But the sun's force was too strong for my mother, who complained of the heat and moved into the shade. By the time we reached home she was suffering from a fierce headache. A touch of sunstroke, we thought. She had formerly had a slight attack in India.

Next morning she was no better, but she insisted on going to the Mortimer Halls and starting to examine the students. She continued all week, the pain getting steadily worse, and by the following Monday she had to admit defeat. She returned home, leaving me to continue the examinations.

She consulted her specialist the next day. The pain seemed most acute in a nerve behind her eye. X-rays were taken and before long a diagnosis was given. There was a secondary

Zest for Life

malignant growth at the top of her spine and she had only a few
months to live.

She had scribbled a letter in pencil to me headed *Prunella – to
be opened in case of emergency*. I tore open the envelope and read it.
It was dated Saturday, 7 July 1934, and headed *Business*.

Prunella,

If this head gets worse and I can't think clearly – stand by the
teachers and the students, see that they get a square deal –
train the ones I have chosen until 1935 – one more year and
then you are free to do what you choose and go where you
will – the League will be safe with about a hundred teachers
to carry its message of Peace and co-operation to all ends of
the earth. . . .

On a separate sheet she had written:

Prunella darling, if my eye is the beginning of my neck giving
further trouble – you have always been my *perfect comfort* and
I know Daddy is proud of you. All my deepest love, my
darling, we have had a marvellous life together.

Mummie

In the months that followed my mother remained at home
among her family. One of her sisters, Nan, Charlie or Norah,
was with her most of the time. She was too ill to receive any
other visitors and she could not read the cards and letters that
poured in from League members. For from the second day of
her illness she was blind.

She listened gratefully to their messages and her concern for
the League's success was as eager as ever, but that era of
ceaseless activity was now at an end. The world she woke to
each day was sightless and pain-filled. She accepted it, never
complaining and never giving up hope.

A number of new centres were due to open that autumn and I
took my mother's place at the inaugural meetings. I also went
to the League headquarters each day, where the prime concern
of everyone was to keep things running as she would have
wished. I reported each detail to her and realized how long she

had been training me for such a contingency. All along, she must have known.

In the evenings, if I was not out on League business, I sat by her bed and we talked – not about her suffering, but often about my father, her days in India and her early family life. It seemed that she was drawing together all the threads of her existence so that I could see the whole pattern. Then she would tire, wait for her nightly injection of morphia, and sink back on her pillows. I would hold her hand, sitting very quietly, hardly breathing, until I knew she had fallen asleep.

At first I dared to think she might recover. But as the months passed I saw more and more clearly that there was no hope. All I could realistically expect was to be allowed to spend some time alone with her for a short while. Such an opportunity presented itself at Christmas. She had been acutely ill just before, but she rallied miraculously and we spent several days together. Outside it was dark and cold, but in her room I felt the same light and warmth that I had always known with her.

We talked about my future and the future of the League. She spoke of my father and the mountains they had loved. 'I knew such perfect happiness in Lansdowne,' she said. 'The Himalayas seemed to express beauty in the deepest sense. Your father and I both felt it. Later, after the war, I tried somehow to work for peace. Because of what he meant to me. Because of the shattering effect of war on so many lives, not just my own.'

In the last weeks, her body seemed divorced from her spirit, which waited to be freed. She died on 15 January 1935 aged fifty-one.

At Christmas I had written a letter to the League members, telling them about her sacrifice. It was published in the New Year edition of the League magazine. Now they all knew. They crowded into the remembrance service we held for her at All Souls' Church, coming from all parts of Britain to lay their flowers beside the wreath of Flanders poppies on her coffin.

I felt very strongly that at last she was released. The peace which she had sought for others for so long was now hers. Its strength and beauty filled the church.

8

Expanding Horizons

The borrowed two years which my mother gave to the League were enough to ensure its survival. Now it could exist without her. We missed her tremendously, but the foundation she had laid was strong enough to guarantee further growth. And there was no lack of devotion or desire to achieve this.

Uppermost in everyone's mind was the conviction that the League must continue. Mollie had 'left' it to me and to her sister Norah. She had trained me as her successor, to be the figurehead of the movement, but I was ably supported by an enthusiastic group of teachers, organizers and grass-roots members, and the continuity of the League depended as much on them as upon my leadership.

Aunt Norah had worked closely with my mother as her confidante and as Editor of the magazine. It was she who now decided that the League should discover what else was going on in the field of physical recreation. Up till then, it had been rather isolated.

At this stage of its existence, the League was viewed askance by most of the physical education professionals. People suspected that Mrs Bagot Stack and her daughter were making a fortune out of their organization. Its popular appeal, the support of the press, the smart exercise uniforms and use of contemporary music were all looked on with suspicion.

The experts of the women's physical training world came from the Women's Colleges of Physical Education, which also supplied the women Physical Training Inspectors, attached to local authorities throughout the country. These colleges had a proud tradition stretching back to Madame Osterberg, who founded the first at Dartford in 1895. Her students were trained in the Ling system of exercises, introduced by her from Sweden, where it had been devised by Per Henrik Ling in the early years of the century and practised by both men and women. Madame Osterberg added games to her curriculum and produced gymnastic teachers who took their place in girls' schools throughout the country. They were models for their pupils in the virtues of 'good temper under trying conditions, courage and determination to play up and do your best, rapidity of thought and action, and self-reliance'.* Pioneers in the development of team games, the women were addressed by their surnames throughout their training and differed little from their brothers in their belief in healthy outdoor exercise as a means of developing character. The Ling system of exercises was a scientific and highly regimented form of body training. It made use of expensive gymnasium equipment – parallel bars, 'horses' to jump over, and ropes to climb up – and contained no recreative or artistic element.

By 1935 there were five Women's Colleges of Physical Education and their graduates held influential positions and advised the Board of Education. It was going to be hard for the League to break through such an entrenched closed shop.

In the dance world, co-operation was much easier. The *Dancing Times* had already given space to articles by Mollie, and Majorie Duncombe's work had the warm approval of Ruby Ginner and her School of Dance and Drama. In the medical world, also, the League had gained approval. Many doctors sent their patients to classes, although the British Medical Association, in the report of a Committee of Inquiry set up to investigate physical training at this time, made no mention of the 1,200 nation-wide health classes operated by the League each week. Aunt Norah felt that the League now deserved to be recognized as a national organization. If this was to come about it must gain the approval of the Board of Education and contacts must be made with officials in the physical training world. She set about pursuing this objective with tact and enthusiasm.

Meantime, I was preparing for the League's largest display

* Sheila Fletcher, *Women First*, Athlone Press, London, 1984.

yet, to be held in May 1935 at Olympia, the building which housed the Royal Military Tournament each year. It was our greatest challenge to date. Would we fill those tiers of spectator seats and recruit enough performers to flood the immense arena?

In the event, *House Full* notices went up outside Olympia long before the evening performance; 2,500 members crowded into the arena to exercise; Marjorie Duncombe contributed a 'Storm Ballet' and Joan St Lo choreographed a spectacular cabaret number. The finale, a moving tribute to my mother, convinced us all that her work would continue.

Later that year the League moved overseas – to Australia, Hong Kong and Canada. It was already established in Eire. I had travelled to Dublin for the opening meeting in the autumn of 1934. The teacher there was Kathleen O'Rourke who had qualified as a gymnast from the I.M. Marsh College of Physical Education, Liverpool, before taking a postgraduate course at the Bagot Stack Health School. Kathleen greeted me with some uncompromising news.

'We've had to make changes,' she said. 'The authorities were suspicious of the word "beauty". So now we're called Ireland's League of Health. And they insist we wear skirts over our short pants when demonstrating in public.'

She went on to tell me that she had arranged for me to meet the Reverend MacQuaid, a cousin of hers, later to become Archbishop of Dublin, who was influential in the Church. 'He'll ask you some stern questions,' she warned, 'but we must get his approval. The attitude of the Church is important.'

My interview with this priest was one of the most searching of my life. Every one of my opinions (most of them intuitive rather than intellectual) was taken apart, scrutinized and then subjected to Christian ethics.

'You are building healthy bodies,' he said. 'For what? You encourage beauty as an aim. Why? Nature, the cultivation of a perfect physique, can never be more than a means to an end. What *is* your end, and how does it correspond to the teaching of the Church?'

It was the first time that beliefs I had taken for granted were cross-examined. I convinced Father MacQuaid of my sincerity, but not, I'm afraid, of a corresponding intellectual rigour.

In spite of this, Ireland's League of Health was successfully launched and has continued to thrive ever since, recently celebrating its fiftieth anniversary.

In the late summer of 1935 Thea Stanley-Hughes, one of Mollie's most promising pupils, sailed to Australia and started classes and a training school for teachers in Sydney. She, too, discarded the word 'beauty' and concentrated on the remedial side of her work, taking pupils recommended by doctors and setting up a structure of continual care for them with the opportunity of classes every day.

Kathleen Glover, newly qualified in July 1935, took the League to Hong Kong; and two British teachers, Natalie Platner and Delphine Solon, travelled to Canada to make preparations for launching the League there.

In September I followed them to speak at the inaugural meeting in Toronto. I found on my arrival that they had already enrolled 138 members. They had demonstrated at the Canadian National Exhibition, in Toronto, which had aroused much interest. As a result, over two thousand women came to the meeting. The Canadians proved to be one of the most receptive audiences we had ever encountered. They were entertained by the exercise sequences, listened in rapt silence when I explained the point of them, watched appreciately as we performed Greek and tap dances, and finally stormed the platform, many of them asking to be enrolled as members right away. That night 146 joined and many more became members once classes started. Toronto was League mad. The enthusiasm was such that the following year a team of Canadians came to England for the second Olympia display and took part with 5,000 British members.

After the Toronto meeting I was able to relax for a few days at a log cabin retreat of some friends near one of the great lakes. I heard there the news of Mussolini's invasion of Abyssinia, an act of naked aggression that was to precede many more. Far from England, it was alarming to feel that another war might be imminent.

The year 1935 was drawing to a close. It had been one of momentous events for the League. In spite of the death of its

founder, sixty-four new centres had opened in Britain and three
overseas. Our great display in Olympia had been successful
and Aunt Norah had made much progress with her plan for
national recognition. The League was beginning to take its
place alongside other forms of physical training.

Scandinavia had always been foremost in that field, and the
Swedish Ling system was widely known in Britain. However,
we did not yet know much of what else was going on in Europe.
In Germany and Italy fitness training was beginning to be used
for military ends, but at the same time it provided many
athletic opportunities for young people. And in Czechoslovakia
the Sokol movement which had inspired my mother still
flourished. There was much of interest to see. So at the end of
1936 Aunt Norah and I decided that I should take two months
off and travel to the Continent to visit several countries and
look at their systems of physical education.

Germany was my first stop. I stayed in Munich with a
German girl who was training with us at the Bagot Stack
Health School. Earlier in 1936 Hitler had marched unopposed
into the Rhineland, started to re-arm it, and thus set the pattern
for future territorial take-overs. His policies, his mass rallies
and his emphasis on compulsory fitness were viewed with grave
suspicion in Britain.

I reached Munich during the Christmas season. Its wide
streets were hung with Nazi flags, side by side with festive
decorations. The churches were filled with worshippers, the
sports grounds with young men and women practising
athletics, playing games or attending compulsory parades.

A German friend, Vicki, entertained me with great
hospitality, and in her house and the homes of her friends I
found no strain. But outside, the Nazi regime was in total
control, its confident propaganda giving an impression of
spectacular social achievement. It was easy to be misled by this
façade, until one realized that physical education was being
used for sinister political purposes.

I was free to view whatever I wanted to, and later in Berlin I
saw a number of different systems of physical training,
including that of Rudolf Laban. His method of dance, dating
from the pre-Nazi period, extolled the value of the individual
and of free expression. His school in Berlin and that of his pupil

Mary Wigman in Dresden still existed. Both continued to exert an influence. Their classes freed the creativity of their pupils, in direct contrast to the regimentation of the state outside their studio walls.

The system I liked best was that of Heinrich Medau, a former colleague of Laban, who trained students and pupils at his Medau School of Gymnastics in Berlin. I studied with him for a while and felt for myself the subtle rhythm and flow of the Medau movement, neither dance nor exercise but something in between; something which used the whole body and awakened the spirit, specially when accompanied by his own wonderful improvised music. Later, at the League's invitation, he and his wife, one of his best exponents, came to London and he taught at a League Teachers' Refresher Course, afterwards appearing on television with some of the girls he had trained.

From Germany I moved on to Czechoslovakia to see the Sokols, who had inspired my mother. They, too, held mass displays of physical training, even larger than the Germans (some numbered 14,000), but theirs was a free democratic organization, founded on Slav traditions and run with discipline but also with a sense of fraternity and co-operation. Prague was a beautiful city and I was warmly welcomed by the Sokols. Later, when the Nazi threat of invasion loomed over Czechoslovakia, I got desperate letters from some of them, pleading for me to help them leave the country. Once again their freedom, so hard won, was to be taken away from them.

I returned to England full of enthusiasm for what I had seen, but met with a luke-warm response. Approved methods of physical training had a strong hold; vested interests had to be defended, and in official quarters only what was 'made in England' was acceptable.

However, the League's mass appeal to women was attracting rival classes. Keep-fit classes had started. Based on the Swedish Ling system, which the Board of Education approved of and supported in the schools, they were financed by local education authorities. Their teachers mostly came from the Women's Colleges of Physical Education, although some of the doyens there disapproved of keep-fit. One, Dr Anna Broman, niece of Madame Osterberg, wrote in the *Journal of School Hygiene and Physical Education*: 'The Keep-Fit movement may have very far-reaching results. . . . We must, indeed, we shall be forced, to make it sound. . . . It is you gymnasts, you educationally trained gymnasts, who can save this reckless and uneducated enthusiasm for something real, something genuine, something fine.'*

But this 'reckless, uneducated enthusiasm' already had its own momentum. By 1936 League membership was close to 100,000. As a pioneer, it had forged a pattern and shown a new approach. This was now amplified in the creation of the Central Council of Recreative Physical Training which was started in 1936 by Phyllis Colson, an old student of the Bedford College of Physical Education. The Council, which had the support of the Board of Education and the specialized Women's Colleges, aimed to draw into its fold all forms of sport, dance and physical training. The League accepted an invitation to join it and has worked in co-operation with it ever since. It later became the Central Council of Physical Recreation, under royal patronage, and helped to transform the concept of physical recreation in Britain.

Influenced by these developments, and by the disquieting emphasis on fitness in the dictator countries, the government woke up to the fact that Britain was physically far from being an A1 nation and decided to do something about it. In May 1937 it appointed a Fitness Council to improve the health of the people and I was asked to join it.

'I do not think it is going too far', wrote the Prime Minister, Stanley Baldwin, in his invitation, 'to say that the success of the Scheme may well depend on the suitability of the personnel of the Council, and I tender to you a very cordial invitation to serve as a member. Your knowledge and experience will, I am confident, prove of the greatest assistance to the Council.'

Of course I accepted! It was a flattering invitation for a 22-year-old, and also a tribute to the League's standing. A series of official engagements and receptions followed and I spoke for the Fitness Council at a number of meetings. The members of the Council were drawn from a variety of professions; these included sportsmen and sportswomen,

---

* *Women First* by Sheila Fletcher.

politicians, civil servants, education authorities and representatives of youth organizations. Margaret Morris and I were the only dancers and we soon found ourselves overwhelmed with memoranda prepared by various government departments. Imagination and inspiration were in short supply, smothered by the bureaucracy of the Civil Service and the Board of Education, under whose aegis we operated. But I did gain valuable experience of working side by side with male colleagues in a wider field, trying to contribute ideas from a woman's perspective. They talked about creating playing fields, sports complexes and gymnasia. But who was to make these facilities come alive? Leaders with vision and enthusiasm would be essential to make them work.

During all this time I sadly missed my mother. In the League I was close to her public persona and I was glad that I could help to continue her work. But when its demands ceased, and I returned alone to Holland Park, I longed for her loving private presence and the confidences and jokes we had shared. It was only two years since her death, even though so much had happened that it seemed longer. Although I could immerse myself in her work, nothing could replace our close relationship. At least that is what I thought, but at that moment fate was preparing a new commitment for me.

In the summer of 1937 the League performed in two huge displays at Wembley Stadium. The first was a Coronation Pageant which it organized on 12 June (its founder's birthday). Five thousand members from 240 centres took part, including a team of sixty-eight from Canada and representatives from Hong Kong, New York and Denmark. The second took place three weeks later. It was a Festival of Youth, sponsored by the Fitness Council and presided over by the newly crowned King George VI and his Queen, Elizabeth. Nine hundred League members performed a display and afterwards I was taken to an ante-room and presented to the royal couple.

Standing at one side was a tall, dark young man whom I recognized as Lord David Douglas-Hamilton, youngest son of the Duke of Hamilton. I had met him and his eldest brother a few weeks before and remembered him as a challenging personality, reserved yet forthright, interested in fitness as I was, but possibly more inclined to consider its wider benefits. We talked, and he invited me to spend a weekend at another brother's house in Hampshire. I accepted, and from that weekend sprang a relationship that was to change my life.

While it was developing I continued to work hard for the League. In the summer of 1938 I made another short trip to the Continent, taking a team of League teachers and members to Hamburg and to Finland. In both places we performed at Physical Training Congresses.

In Hamburg, the huge spectacular arena displays were organized by the Nazis with blaring propaganda and meticulous discipline. Specialist teams like our own showed their work at small halls and theatres; but all participants joined together in the opening ceremony in the arena and a subsequent march through the city streets. The British contingent received, it seemed to me, a specially warm welcome from the people lining the route; once again I was struck by the contrast between the regimentation of the Nazi regime and the spontaneous reaction of individual Germans when an opportunity arose to show their feelings.

A huge *Kraft durch Freude* (Strength through Joy) luxury liner was moored alongside the quay in Hamburg's port. It accommodated thirty-two different foreign teams, including our own; and after the Congress all these teams were taken on a cruise to Lisbon and Madeira. Groups of favoured German workers were offered similar holidays throughout the year as a reward for good party behaviour, but none of them were on this particular trip, which was reserved for foreigners.

I waved our team goodbye and then, with Peggy and Joan St Lo, flew to Denmark and we all three boarded a boat to sail across the Baltic to Helsinki. As we sped over the northern waves I reflected on how far we had come together since our days in my mother's children's class. The work we had learnt then had now been extended to many countries, the latest being New Zealand where League classes had recently started up. We had demonstrated our system of exercises in Germany and now we were on our way to show it in Scandinavia, where we would meet other continental colleagues and have an opportunity to exchange information and ideas. I knew that this international aspect of her work would have delighted my mother. If only she could have been with us to share it!

In Finland we saw much of interest. The representatives from Lithuania, Latvia and Estonia performed a graceful flowing type of movement new to us and quite different from the Swedish Ling system. (Like Czechoslovakia, these countries were soon to be absorbed by a powerful neighbour, in this case Russia.) We also made friends with a Danish team from Copenhagen and a Medau team from Berlin, both of whom gave excellent displays and promised to visit us in England the following year.

The Helsinki Congress, called the *Suomen Voimistelun Suursikat*, was organized by a group of women's societies. Their friendly welcome and simple, unpretentious hospitality showed us international fellowship free from propaganda or state control. Perhaps one day, I thought, we would be able to hold a similar convention in our own country.

But soon after my return, anxiety about the immediate future put all such hopes out of my mind. Britain was plunged into the Munich crisis. Faced with the choice of betraying Czechoslovakia or, ill-prepared and unwilling, going to war with Hitler, the nation was deeply divided. Peace hung in the balance. The Prime Minister, Neville Chamberlain, flew to Munich and returned waving his famous piece of paper and assuring us of 'peace in our time'. But the conflict had only been postponed.

During the crisis League headquarters was threatened with being commandeered for a casualty clearing station. This gave us a foretaste of the future. I tried to come to terms with the threat that hung over my mother's life-work. If war came, all that she had striven for might perish. Of what use then would be one individual's ideals and sacrifice? The Nazi evil must be resisted and perhaps only force could overcome it. I knew this, but I remembered also my mother's experience of war and the irretrievable loss my father's death had brought.

It seemed that now some of Mollie's vision for her League was being fulfilled: its huge membership, its expansion abroad, its international contacts. However, her vision of it as a force for world peace seemed increasingly remote.

We had one more year of peace. The League was flourishing. It now occupied all four floors of the premises my mother had secured with such optimism. One hundred teachers were being trained and more than two thousand classes ran throughout the country each week. Membership had risen to 166,000.

The League still suffered from financial problems. Its expansion had brought mounting expense. There was no money in reserve; for the only income came from members' subscriptions and class fees, sufficient to just cover running costs but no more. However, the League now received national recognition from the Fitness Council, who offered it a grant of £6,000 if a matching sum could be raised from the League's own resources. Members responded generously to an Appeal Fund for this purpose and the Council's Chairman, Lord Aberdare, wrote:

> Thank you for the support which the League has given to the National Fitness Campaign. Your own beautifully staged demonstrations have, I am confident, led to a much wider appreciation of what fitness means. Your members in different parts of the country have contributed to the success of many local demonstrations arranged by National Fitness Committees and at public meetings your displays have given point to speeches on National Fitness. Prunella has not only helped by her membership of the Council and its Committees, but has been one of our leading speakers. For all this the Fitness cause owes you much.

Meanwhile, preparations were going ahead for another huge League display at Wembley Stadium, this time an International Festival. Invitations were sent to ten European countries asking them to join in the opening ceremony and perform items of their own. The St Los and I planned a spectacular production in honour of our foreign guests. A team of sixty would be present from Canada and so would representatives from Ireland (North and South), Australia, New York and Hong Kong. At last, it seemed, we could truly demonstrate my mother's aim – 'Health, leading to Peace.'

But in March 1939 the Nazis invaded Czechoslovakia. Hitler's speeches became ever more strident and the international climate so precarious that most of the continental teams we invited were unable to come. The display reverted to an Empire Pageant of Health and Beauty. Even so, 6,000 League members participated. And their performance on the green grass of Wembley's vast arena, lit by a mellow sun and later, as darkness fell, by dramatic spotlights, remained in the memory of many of the thousands who thronged the auditorium to watch them on that June evening in the last summer of peace.

I had one more chance to visit Europe. A world Physical Education Training Congress – the *Lingiad* – was held in Stockholm in July 1939 to celebrate the centenary of Per Henrik Ling, founder of Swedish gymnastics. The National Fitness Council sponsored British representation and asked the League to go. We sent twenty young teachers who took their place beside teams from the specialist Physical Education Colleges and several other voluntary organizations. In typical British fashion, we were a motley collection, each with a different system, different exercise kit and different aims. But we were democratic, although we nursed fierce rivalries. None of the others had thought of wearing a travelling uniform; so our contingent, all in their early twenties, arriving in Stockholm in smart white dresses, with fetching white bandeaus, stole most of the publicity.

We took part in the Ceremony of Opening when teams from all the Scandinavian countries, and from Iceland, Poland, Portugal, Romania, Hungary, Germany and Greece marched past the King of Sweden. We showed our own work in a demonstration at Stockholm's large Concert House; and we watched the massed arena displays of the Swedes and the Germans, the latter sunburnt to an identical brown from their cruise to Stockholm on their *Kraft durch Freude* ship. Hitler had sent 1,000 participants – 500 men and 500 women. No fraternization was allowed. The Germans were marched straight from the ship to the arena and then straight back again after their performance. But a few select teams from other nations were invited on board, ours among them. And one evening we attended a dance where some of our girls taught their partners to tap-dance and were reproved for passing on such decadent practices to the pure German youth.

On the last night of the Congress all the teams, except the Germans, crowded into Stockholm's beautiful golden City Hall for a banquet and a dance. The peasant dresses with their splashes of colour, the flags, the dancing, the music and the laughter all combined to create a joyous atmosphere. There were no barriers between these people. Everyone was spontaneously happy, living for the moment, although that moment was an evening in late July 1939.

I tried to describe this experience when I returned to Scotland and talked to the students at a Fitness Summer School in the Highlands, organized by David Douglas-Hamilton. There, too, I found the harmony of a group of people united in a common interest, free from political differences or prejudice. The Summer School ended in late August. On 1 September Hitler marched into Poland. Two days later Britain's Prime Minister declared war on Germany. And on 3 September 1939 our nation began a new existence.

In those first days I often thought of my mother. Her war had started in a far country, thousands of miles from home. Almost at once it had entailed intense personal loss. Mine began in familiar surroundings, but within them everything changed. Streets and houses were immediately blacked out. Barrage balloons hung like puffs of cloud above the city. Posters went up warning against careless talk. Gas-masks and ration books were issued. Enemy aliens were interned. People everywhere gravitated towards the services or towards war employment. And the banshee wail of air-raid sirens alarmed us all.

During the Munich crisis Aunt Norah and I had approached various Ministries to see if any of the League personnel could be employed in war service. The answer was no, not unless the individual concerned had trained for the job and possessed the necessary qualifications. The League was a peacetime organization with peacetime aims. In war, it was redundant. Its teachers were forced to turn to other employment. Many of them joined the Women's Services and brought their expertise with them, conducting classes for Forces personnel wherever they happened to be. Many of the members did the same, or became nurses, munition workers, air-raid wardens, or minders of evacuees.

In London, Peggy and Joan St Lo continued classes at the League headquarters, but before long the building had to be evacuated. They then carried on in various halls, moving from one to the next as raids reduced central London to rubble. Brave and loyal League members followed them, and throughout the war they maintained a nucleus for centres throughout the country.

As time passed, the classes that the League still managed to provide gave welcome relief to women exhausted by war duties as well as the burden of raids, evacuees, clothes and food rationing and constant anxiety for their men on active service. In their black-and-white exercise kit, members went through the familiar routines, and forgot for a while the pressures of war. They laughed, relaxed, made friends and restored their energy once more.

In some centres teachers were able to combine their teaching with another job. In others, when teachers were called up, advanced members took their place, receiving extra training at courses specially organized for them. A nucleus of fifty centres remained open, held together by a determination that the League's work should survive and reinforced by an annual Teachers' Refresher Course, which as many girls as possible attended, even if it meant sacrificing precious service leave.

When war came I was in a position where I could no longer devote my whole life to the League.

I had met David Douglas-Hamilton in the summer of 1937 and this had added a new dimension to my life. For the rest of that year we saw a lot of each other. I stayed at his home in Scotland, we climbed mountains together in Skye and in the Alps, and I helped him prepare for a Fitness Summer School run in the Highlands during August 1938 by the Scottish Fitness Council who appointed him as Warden.

As well as sharing my interests, David stimulated my mind and gave me a larger conception of my work. Conversations

with him sometimes reminded me of the Irish priest who had
challenged my beliefs in Dublin. David had read politics,
philosophy and economics (then called Modern Greats) at
Oxford, and he had a considerable grasp of world affairs. He
knew both Germany and Russia well and observed Hitler's
increasing power with dismay. Behind an outward façade of
irony David had a deep idealism and a real desire to be of
service to the community. This was tempered by a keen sense of
humour. He was not above teasing me about my 'life-work', the
League.

We fell in love. But when it came to the question of marriage,
doubts loomed. He and I came from very different back-
grounds.

'My radical Aunt Nan thinks I'd be letting down the family
by marrying into the aristocracy!' I told him.

David laughed. 'That's just inverted snobbery,' he replied. 'I
agree with Robbie Burns. "A man's a man for a' that." Have
you ever felt embarrassed or out of place with my family?'

'Never.'

'Well, then. . . .'

'But what about my League work?'

'You know I'd want you to continue that. You're lucky to
have such a fine organization behind you. Of course you must
go on leading it.'

In the end it was our hearts, not our heads, which impelled
us. By the spring of 1938 we were engaged, and we planned to
marry that autumn. The Munich crisis intervened. We almost
put our wedding forward when war seemed certain, but in the
event we were able to stick to the original date of 15 October.

We were married in Glasgow Cathedral. A special train ran
from London to accommodate friends, family and League
teachers and members, who travelled up to Scotland overnight
and swelled the number of guests in the cathedral to a
thousand. At the reception afterwards David responded to the
bridal toast by inviting all present to visit us 'when we are
settled in our wee but-an-ben'. This proved to be a house in
London where we lived for the next year.

David was a member of the Royal Air Force Volunteer
Reserve. When war came he was called up immediately. But he
was not yet on active service. I was able to follow him to the

various stations where he completed his flying training. When that ended, he was posted as an instructor to a Fleet Air Arm Flying Training School in Wiltshire and we lived together in a house nearby. Our eldest son, Diarmaid, was born on the day that France fell, 17 June 1940, and he narrowly escaped the first great London raid on 7 September. I had taken him there so that I could attend a League Teachers' Refresher Course, which ended only the day before the raid.

From our home in Wiltshire we watched the Battle of Britain raging in the skies; later heard with horror what was happening to London. My Aunt Nan was running a clothing factory there in the East End, producing battle-dress uniforms for the army and refusing to leave while she had this important war work to do. Aunt Norah had died the day after my son was born in a car accident. Her loss was a sad one for the League. She had helped to steer it through the difficult months after my mother's death and taken the first steps towards getting it recognized as a national movement. Now, with teachers and members scattered, the preservation of the magazine which she had edited was vital for the future. I took on this task and managed to produce a slim volume four times a year throughout the war.

Although in September 1939 no one dreamt of honour and glory as they had in 1914, most people felt a sense of patriotism, resolution and a determination to see the war through to the end. But as the years passed, the war consumed more and more of people's hope.

I often thought of the friends I had made in Europe and wondered how they were faring. An unbridgeable gulf separated us. I knew that many of them must be suffering from hunger, homelessness, imprisonment and the horrors of invasion – war at first hand, worse than anything that had yet touched Britain. But I was powerless to help. Where now were hopes of international friendship and understanding?

David was chafing at his safe instructor's job in the Flying Training School. At last, in November 1941, he got his dearest wish and was transferred to a fighter squadron – the City of Edinburgh, 603 – which was operating at Hornchurch, near London. I stayed nearby, and then followed him to Dyce, in

Aberdeenshire, where he took over the leadership of the squadron when his commanding officer was lost on a flight across the North Sea. But our days together were numbered. In early April 1942 the squadron was posted overseas. David sailed under sealed orders, just as my father had done so many years ago, and then led his squadron off the American aircraft carrier on which they had travelled and across the hostile Mediterranean to Malta. I went to live in his mother's house in Dorset, where soon my second baby would be born.

In the peace of the country, with farm milk from Jersey cows, home-grown vegetables and a big house packed with evacuated children, it was difficult to imagine bombed London or hard-pressed Malta. David was living under seige conditions. Huge enemy raids from Sicily continually harassed the island. Supplies, impossible to reinforce, were running low. The few Spitfire squadrons available attacked formations of German Junkers 88s four times their size, and their strength was reduced each day by casualties that could not be replaced. In his letters David told me some of this. He minimized the danger, but I knew he was stretched to his limit.

On 16 August 1942 my second son, Iain, was born. I survived the long night thinking of David, with no certainty that he was still alive. Then, miraculously, a few days later he turned up in England, safe and sound although a stone lighter! He delivered an important message to the Air Ministry and then raced to Dorset, bringing with him a bunch of bananas for Diarmaid, the first the child had ever seen.

David had a few weeks' leave and then was transferred to a ground job for a while to recover from the strain of Malta. But he was determined to return to operations as soon as he could. He succeeded in doing this in June 1943 when he joined a photographic reconnaissance squadron and was trained to fly Mosquitoes on long trips across occupied Europe. This reconnaissance work was vital for the Second Front, soon to be launched, and also important for the detection of secret weapons planned to terrorize the civilian population of Britain.

All the pilots who flew Mosquitoes loved them. Their engines were tuned up to achieve great height and speed, their only protection, for they were unarmed and frequently exposed to enemy fire. Their missions were unpredictable and dangerous. Pilots were lost through temperamental engine failure as well as from enemy action.

David was based at Benson aerodrome in Oxfordshire. He could come home for some weekends, but as the months passed the strain of operations took its toll and he grew thinner and increasingly preoccupied by the war. Raids had started again in London; now the city was being bombarded by flying bombs, whose base at Pienemunde, in Germany, had first been located by a photographic reconnaissance plane.

In one of these raids my Aunt Nan was killed. She was riding her bicycle down Kensington High Street when the sirens sounded. Before she could take cover, a flying bomb exploded. Death was a familiar visitor in those days, but I could not believe it had claimed Nan. Of the four Irish sisters of whom my mother had told me so much, only one, Charlie, now remained. Nan had been a strong influence on me all my life and a precious link with my mother, to whom she was devoted. I loved her very much for her originality, her mocking independent spirit, her freedom from convention.

I telephoned David to tell him. He had just returned from a long sortie over Germany and was due to fly another one the next day.

'Take care,' I said.

'I'll be fine,' he answered.

But as he flew back from the South of France, his plane was hit. One engine was put out of action and his navigator was severely wounded. He limped back across the Channel and tried to land at Benson. He was in the aerodrome's circuit when his second engine failed. He turned downwind for the only open country, but his wing struck a belt of trees and the plane crashed. He and his navigator were killed. The date was 2 August 1944.

I heard the news at Benson, where I had driven that day to meet him. His plane had crashed only an hour before my arrival. In the first unspeakable shock my mind was numb. 'David, David, David. . . . ' I kept saying to myself. The CO who had just inspected the plane, lying on the edge of the airfield, told me that David must have died instantly.

I thought of my mother. She, too, had received the news of

her husband's death alone among strangers. She had been widowed at thirty-two, I at thirty. Somehow she had survived and had brought me up without a father. Now I would have to do the same for my sons.

9

New Challenges

A year later the war ended. The League had come through with remarkable vitality. Fifty centres were still open, maintained to a large extent by the enthusiasm of their members. Teachers had kept in touch and would soon return from the services, and public recognition was accorded to the League by requests for displays in many parts of the country. The culmination of these took place in London on 23 September 1946 before an audience of 17,000. The *Sunday Graphic* reported next day: 'The main attraction of London's Thanksgivings Week was the League of Health and Beauty Display.'

Joan St Lo had trained a team of members who performed, perched on a platform high above Trafalgar Square, where they showed a spectacular new exercise sequence. I watched them with pride. We had a fine nucleus on which to rebuild. And rebuild we must – quickly.

The physical training scene was undergoing profound change. And the League, instead of being in the vanguard of the women's exercise movement, as in pre-war days, was faced with stiff competition. Keep-fit classes proliferated. They followed the system taught in the Physical Education Colleges, were subsidized by local authorities and approved of by Physical Training Inspectors. Classes were also cheaper than the League's. They trained their own teachers in short courses with grant-aided fees, aiming to produce, not professionals, but competent leaders for their classes. Many women were attracted by this opportunity of part-time training. As often happens, the pioneer's vision – my mother's – had been

149

adopted by others, then diffused and expanded.

In the Physical Education Colleges, too, a fundamental change was taking place. The rigidly enforced doctrines of the Ling system were being challenged by the new concept of free natural movement that I had seen in Germany. Rudolf Laban's system was permeating the Colleges, aided by Lisa Ullman's Art of Movement Studio which opened in Manchester in 1943 and the publication, in 1948, of Laban's book *Modern Educational Dance*. In the late 1940s and early 1950s a revolution took place, and Laban's concepts of weight, space, time and flow replaced the science and precision of Ling.

The new movement was creative and free; self-aware in the realm of the psyche rather than the body. Laban's approach was unrelentingly serious (that, at any rate, it shared with Ling!). But it fitted in with the contemporary feeling for self-expression, released after the regimentation of war, and it had the artistic content for which people hungered in contrast to recent cultural austerity. It was also in line with the new doctrines of education with its emphasis on choice and self-development rather than domination by a teacher from a platform.

The League responded to these changes by occupying a central position between the rigid discipline of Ling and the free concepts of *Modern Educational Dance*. It retained its basic Bagot Stack body training, which required precision and technique, but constantly enlarged its repertoire with new exercise and movement sequences, bearing in mind the ultimate goal of a training in grace and expression.

In 1946, our first priority was the reopening of the Bagot Stack Health School. I travelled to Dublin to persuade Kathleen O'Rourke to come over to England to be its Principal and was delighted when she agreed. I knew that she had exceptional insight into the training of the body, combined with the necessary authority and humour to convey it to others. Students trained by her would learn the remedial and anatomical side of their work in depth. For their movement experience, we asked Molly Braithwaite, now teaching the Medau system in England, to join the staff of the school and she introduced the students to the swinging rhythmic Medau movement, well known in Europe, which they could later adapt for their League classes.

Meanwhile the St Los organized and produced a Peace-Time Rally and Demonstration in Hyde Park followed by a display at the Empire Pool, Wembley, where 1,500 members performed before an audience of 8,000. These events attracted a number of teachers back to the League, where they resumed their work in their old centres, or opened new ones.

We were adapting to the challenge of post-war conditions and realizing that life was more demanding than in the 1930s. Many women were working as well as looking after their homes and children. When they chose a leisure-time activity from the many now available, they wanted something which would produce quick results. Fortunately, the League could meet that demand. It continued to improve the health and physique of its members and to provide exercises within the capacity of the average woman. But the emphasis now was more on benefit to the individual and less on the far-reaching ideals of its founder. My mother's vision of 'Health leading to Peace' had been eclipsed by the war, though the distinctive 'League spirit' of comradeship and enjoyment, which she had fostered, was still manifest in all the classes.

In the financial sphere, the League's problems were no longer so acute. It still had to exist from its own resources without any help from the government or local authorities. But its expenses were far lower. The Treasurer, Torquil Macleod, who had rescued the League finances during the war, had also helped to change the way it was run. It now had four Directors – Torquil Macleod, Peggy St Lo, myself and a representative of the members. There was no longer an expensive headquarters. Peggy was Organizing Secretary, working from her home, and Torquil Macleod's City firm of solicitors provided an office address. Teachers were self-employed, appointed to an area by the Directors and free to develop it as they saw fit. And their expertise soon brought new and old members back into the classes.

After the war I settled into the house David and I had bought in

London, and tried to come to terms with his loss. The two
people I had loved most – David and my mother – had gone.
They left a gap I could not fill. Post-war living brought its own
problems: shortages, rations, weariness, disillusion. David and
I talked at the beginning of the war of 'winning the peace'. But
the six long years had drained away people's vitality and
idealism. Europe was devastated; many of its cities in ruins.
When I remembered my mother's vision for her League, it
seemed to belong to a different age.

Yet the League had survived. And although it was now an
uphill struggle I could continue her work. Pioneer enthusiasm
gave way to an effort to maintain what we had already achieved
and to wait patiently for further development until more new
teachers could be trained. Fortunately the climate of opinion
made expansion easier. Many of my mother's original views on
health were becoming accepted wisdom. Once the exhaustion
of the post-war years had passed, more and more women would
want to put them into practice.

I could relate to my mother through her work but there was
nothing to take David's place. Bringing up our two sons alone
only accentuated his loss. They so often reminded me of him;
little resemblances in character or physique which were
infinitely poignant. Yet they brought me down to earth. Their
needs and demands pointed to the future, not the past. And
their robust vitality and curiosity had to be satisfied. David's
family remained close to me, a precious reminder of him.

During this time the boys went to a nursery school in
Kensington, near our house, and then the eldest was old
enough to leave London for a preparatory school in Dorset.

One day, unexpectedly, someone I had known before the war
arrived to see me. He was a South African called Alfred Albers
– Ally for short. I had met him at Oxford in 1936 when he was a
Rhodes Scholar at Oriel College studying medicine and we had
become great friends. Later, David entered my life and took his
place, but we still kept in touch. I knew he had joined the Royal
Army Medical Corps and served in the Italian campaign. Now
he was in London studying at Guy's Hospital for his Fellowship
of the Royal College of Surgeons.

An old friend can revive joy. Ally and I knew one another so
well that there was no need for pretence. His cheerfulness and

simplicity brought a new element into my life. I began to believe that there could still be happiness ahead. We ski'ed together in the Alps, climbed in the Dolomites, and he became my children's greatest friend, full of adventurous and imaginative ideas. Late in 1949 he travelled back to South Africa, where he planned to live permanently and to practise medicine as a specialist. And I had to decide whether I wanted to follow him. Could I leave my work, my country and my friends, and take my children to a foreign land where they would be educated and brought up far from their family and its traditions?

Ally insisted that I should visit Cape Town before making up my mind. So in the spring of 1950 I boarded a ship and sailed over the sea to the southern tip of Africa. The Cape produced a conflict of impressions – beauty, squalor, luxury, injustice, friendliness, resentment. How could I trust myself and my sons to this disturbing new environment? It was a difficult decision. But in the end Ally himself became the deciding factor. Once again, my heart showed me the way. I promised to marry him.

Back in England I spent a hectic few months packing up my house, preparing the children for the move and dealing with my responsibilities to the League. Two important things had happened. In 1949 the Bagot Stack Health School had been transferred to a studio in Holland Park, next door to the house where it began. It was flourishing, with a set of keen students and a Principal, Marnel King, who had been trained by Ruby Ginner and was also a successful League teacher. I saw the students regularly and conducted a weekly class in public speaking for them. In 1950 the League, under the guidance of Torquil Macleod, had changed its constitution to that of a non-profit-making association with charity status, governed by a council. I approached a number of distinguished people to serve on this: among them Lord Aberdare of the Fitness Council, Sir Noel Curtis-Bennett, Chairman of the National Playing Fields Association, Brigadier T.H. Wand-Tetley, former Chairman of the Army Physical Training School, Miss K. Curlett, director of the Girls' Training Corps, and Professor M.L. Jacks, Director of the Department of Education at Oxford University. Its first Chairman was the judge Sir Cyril Atkinson (an old friend of my mother's and a lifelong supporter of her work); he was followed at a later date by Lord Sempill, another Council member.

The League now had a thousand weekly classes running in Britain, overseas centres in Eire, Canada, Australia and New Zealand, an efficient Executive Committee, and money in the bank at last. The new Association had started with capital of £1,000, a very satisfactory sum then, donated from previous League funds. I was confident that it would continue successfully in Britain and, sad though I was to leave it, I hoped I could expand its activities by taking it to South Africa.

So, at its twentieth Birthday celebration at the Empire Pool, Wembley, in May 1950, I said *au revoir* to my League colleagues and friends; and in June my sons and I boarded the SS *Edinburgh Castle* and set sail for South Africa, taking with us two dogs, a Siamese cat and a sheaf of farewell telegrams.

Ally and I were married in Cape Town Cathedral on 22 July 1950. We settled in an area called Constantia, fifteen miles outside the city, in a house surrounded by vineyards with a fine view of the Table Mountain massif. With my sons, now aged ten and eight, we climbed on the mountain, camped beside white sandy beaches, dived into huge Cape breakers, and watched constellations wheel across the southern sky. Then, holidays over, the boys departed for their new preparatory school, Ally continued with his medical practice, and I was left to adjust myself to the leisurely Cape.

I was homesick. How could I integrate with this strange community, imbued with suburban values and racial prejudice? I had nothing to give to it except my work. How could I start that, and where was it most needed?

I drove down to District Six, the area where the Cape Coloureds (people of mixed blood, half black, half white) lived. They were crowded into small houses in narrow streets, segregated from the whites, but with a vital life of their own, although their area was reputed to be one of the worst in the city for crime and disturbance. On my previous trip to Cape Town I had visited District Six with Ally and we had addressed a large school there run by Dr Golding, a leader of the coloured community. He had introduced me to Mrs Roman, warden of a hostel at Zonnebloem College, where coloured students trained as nurses and teachers, several of them coming from other parts of South Africa. Mrs Roman had asked me to take a class for her girls. I now contacted her and the class began.

The students were shy at first but had a natural talent for movement, and once I had gained their confidence they responded marvellously. After three months of classes they had progressed enough to give a short display. They invited their friends to an 'at home' at the College and performed what they had learnt, wearing the black-and-white League exercise kit. So the League work was first shown in South Africa by people with dark skins.

The following February, I extended classes to the white community. I held an opening meeting at the City Hall in Cape Town. After a week 300 members had joined. A month later the Zonnebloem girls demonstrated to a large non-European audience in District Six, and that brought sixty-five new recruits to their class.

The enthusiasm of the South African members reminded me of the League's early days. Each lesson was a discovery for them and for me; a revelation of talent. The restrictions of post-war England fell away and I was free to develop my work in any way I chose.

Ally gave me great support, attending the opening meeting at the City Hall and sharing its excitement and success. Like me, he had found it difficult to adjust to life in the Cape. South Africa had changed much since his days there as a schoolboy and an undergraduate. The Nationalist Government had come to power two years previously and was enforcing its policy of apartheid. I was already experiencing this in my classes, where white and coloured members had to be taught separately. Now Ally attended a Medical Meeting which admitted only doctors and specialists with white skins. When Ally pointed out the unfairness and impoverishing effect of this policy he was looked at with suspicion by some of his colleagues. The field of medicine was a highly competitive one and newcomers were not encouraged to air liberal views. This was a different climate of opinion from what he had expected. It would take time for him to find like-minded colleagues.

Nevertheless, the beauty of the Cape remained. Table

Mountain, high above the city, towered magnificent and serene, its 'tablecloth' of filmy mist spilling over its massive crags. Ally had known the mountain all his life but had never rock-climbed on it. We joined the Mountain Club and explored its ridges and precipitous cliff faces. A thousand feet of clean, dry rock was not an unusual climb. Ascending, we sat on ledges, a toy town far below, and watched huge cumulus clouds unfold across the sky as we waited for our turn on the rope. Politics, in such places, belonged to another world.

But Table Mountain could also destroy. Nine months after our marriage, on Easter Saturday 1951, Ally fell on a climb on Table Mountain. We were with two experienced climbers, Sir Evelyn Baring, British High Commissioner in South Africa, and Tom Bright, an expert member of the Mountain Club. We had been traversing a seemingly easy path across a steep cliff face and were unroped when Ally, who was leading, slipped and in one terrible moment fell ninety feet on to the rocks below.

We reached him as soon as we could, and while the other two went for help I sat beside him among the boulders and the heaths. The fierce sun beat down on us, draining the landscape of colour. There was no sound, human or animal, not even wind. Ally was silent too; unconscious, mortally injured, his head pillowed on a rucksack. The moments turned into hours with no water, no shade, no help. And in that silence, under that sun, Ally died.

With Ally's death, my first thought was, Now I can go home. But in the event I stayed on in South Africa. I found I could not so soon leave his country. Although so short, our life together had been happy and constructive. I did not want to squander or destroy its memories. The Cape community and my League members, white and coloured, were wonderfully kind. They wanted me to stay. Perhaps I could still do something for them? So I remained.

I wrote to Peggy St Lo in London and asked her to send me a teacher who would help develop the League in South Africa. I suggested Barbara Keys, a young graduate of the Bagot Stack Health School who was also a dancer with beautiful movement.

She had recently taught League classes in Canada and was now training our students. Peggy agreed with my choice, persuaded Barbara, and in a few months she arrived.

Now began a most satisfying period of my working life. Barbara and I saw eye to eye about introducing free movement into our classes. We had an excellent concert pianist, Estelle de la Ville, who improvised for us; and the South African members responded appreciatively to the creative work we gave them. The coloured girls had a natural grace and rhythm. They showed us some of their African dances and laughed a great deal at our efforts to perform them. And the white members were ready to try anything; they were unselfconscious and uninhibited, in spite of a slight languorousness induced by a hot climate.

Barbara and I took lessons from a teacher who had trained with Martha Graham, the famous American pioneer of modern dance. Unlike Laban, the Graham method included meticulous technique, starting with strenuous floor exercises which limbered every part of the body, particularly the spine. Only when these had been practised did our teacher progress to free movement and leaps. I realised afresh how right my mother had been to insist on her basic body training as a prelude and accompaniment to dance.

Meanwhile in England the young Queen, Elizabeth II, was to be crowned in 1953. The League planned a Coronation Display at the Royal Albert Hall and we were invited to send a team. The project was welcomed enthusiastically by the South African members, and soon we were selecting twenty-eight for the team from the fifty who had volunteered, and making plans to raise money to help with their fares.

We had already given several displays in Cape Town and each time had included items by coloured members. These had to be kept separate from the white items, since the mixing of the races in a public display was forbidden. But now we were taking a group to England, where no colour bar existed. What an opportunity to show the true extent of League work in South Africa!

We assembled our white members and put the idea of a mixed team to them. They seemed amicable to the plan. We selected two girls from the Zonnebloem class called Marjorie

Austin and Mary Williams, who were in their early twenties, both workers in a sweet factory. Then we called the whole group together for the first rehearsal of the item we were developing. It was a series of movements to a rhapsody by Dohnányi and would take six months to learn and perfect.

I expected difficulties from the South African authorities. It was doubtful that Marjorie and Mary would be given passports. But I did not foresee the amount of prejudice that would exist among the white members themselves. Several said their husbands or parents objected to their training or performing with coloured girls, and there was an undercurrent of discontent.

'We'll have to talk to them again,' I said to Barbara.

'Some of them think it will harm the League in South Africa to sponsor a mixed team,' she replied.

'Not so. It will show where we stand,' I declared.

At the next rehearsal, before Marjorie and Mary arrived, we reminded the members of the ideals of the League: that there should exist no barriers of race or class. We told them it had been founded to serve women everywhere, whatever the colour of their skins. 'A mixed team with English-speaking, Afrikaners and coloured members would be truly representative of the League's work in South Africa,' I concluded. Then we took a vote. Two-thirds were in favour. There were still some doubtful faces, but it was agreed that we should go ahead.

Six months later we all set sail for England. The first contingent left on 16 March and I followed with the remainder at the end of April. We had raised £1,000 towards the fares. Our travelling uniform of navy-blue suits with yellow shirts and hats enhanced both dark and light skins. And the final integration of the coloured girls took place at sea when they overcame the last remnants of prejudice among their team-mates by expertly making up the white girls' eyes (as only they knew how), so that they could sparkle provocatively above the yashmaks they wore to the Fancy Dress Ball.

The SS *Edinburgh Castle* was a British ship, with no colour bar. Marjorie and Mary shared a cabin full of flowers and baskets of fruit from their friends in District Six; and when we arrived at Southampton a posse of pressmen photographed the whole team and then took pictures of me flanked by a dark and a light South African, one on each side. That night the *Evening Standard* reported:

> The Women's League of Health and Beauty and their leader, Miss Prunella Stack, have won a victory over Dr Malan's colour bar. Among 28 South African girls who will take part in a display at the Albert Hall later this month are two coloured girls – Miss Mary Williams, aged 20, and Mrs Marjorie Austin, 23. The two girls were among a party of nine who arrived at Southampton today in the *Edinburgh Castle*. Miss Stack was with them. In Cape Town the coloured and white members of the League have separate classes. On board the ship they sat at the same table.

'How proud our Founder would have been of the growth of her work and the inspiration so evident here tonight,' I said, as I gave my opening address at the Albert Hall display. The arena was packed with members from Britain, Eire and Canada. Every seat in the auditorium was full. The South Africans entered down the staircase below the royal box, their yellow tunics gleaming like a burst of sunshine. And when the television cameras recorded their item and focused on Marjorie and Mary exercising with their white compatriots, I knew that the message of a mixed team would be carried to millions of viewers throughout the country.

Later, they all travelled to Edinburgh where they performed in Princes' Street Gardens below the Castle, and were given a civic luncheon by the Lord Provost. Then they went on to Glasgow where they repeated their item for the Scottish members. In London, they saw the Coronation procession and many of them visited the Continent before returning home. It was a trip for them to remember all their lives.

I stayed another three years in South Africa and then, early in 1956, finally made the break with Ally's country and brought my sons home to complete their education at Gordonstoun School in Scotland. I was as sad to go as I had been to leave England six years before. But new work and responsibilities awaited me.

During my absence the League had advanced in the field of social service. Some of the teachers now held classes in hospitals and mental homes, in pre- and post-natal clinics, among the women in Holloway Prison, and for children in Preston's Royal Cross School for the Deaf. This work called for a special kind of dedication, of which not everyone was capable. The teachers who undertook it employed great skill in adapting the League exercises and gaining the confidence of their pupils. The main body of classes continued as before, but there was increasing concern that, in order to equip the young teachers with the skills and qualifications necessary for a satisfactory career in a changing world, the programme of teacher training needed fundamental development.

When I went to South Africa my place on the Executive Committee had been taken by Vickie Gunter. Her husband, the late Professor Francis Aylward, was aware of the facilities in American and European universities for developing and recognizing this aspect of physical education. He outlined a syllabus that would be acceptable to the existing education authorities and approached Morley College, a famous centre of adult education closely linked with drama, music and art, in the hope that the League teacher training might be housed there. Evening classes at Morley were in full swing despite repair work on the damage suffered during the war. But Denis Richards, the Principal, was co-operative and constructive and agreed that the League could become a daily tenant. It could use the Holst Hall and several classrooms. The League Council warmly supported the project, and in September 1955 the teacher training transferred to Morley College, and the Bagot Stack Health School was re-named the Bagot Stack College.

It offered a full-time two-year diploma course, with a syllabus in line with new trends in physical education and dance. Its Principal was Joan Wilder, one of our most valued and experienced teachers who had trained under my mother. She gathered together an impressive staff and, as well as teaching the Bagot Stack system to the students, set it down in a training manual – a very important thing to do.

Morley College, with its special emphasis on music and the arts, was a wonderful venue for the teacher training offered by the League. The London Symphony Orchestra rehearsed there regularly; an Opera School and the Jooss-Leeder School of Modern Dance soon also became day-time tenants; and all operated under the encouraging aegis of Denis Richards, who became a strong supporter of the League's work.

I visited the Bagot Stack College soon after my return from South Africa, and was most impressed with what I saw. Two of my young South African members had joined the course, travelling from Cape Town to spend two years in London. They completed the training successfully, and subsequently one of them, Betty O'Donaghue, opened the League in Johannesburg and Pretoria, where it still flourishes.

As for the League's involvement in social service, this was typical of the more caring attitude to people which the new National Health Service exemplified. In the League, we began to think of a pension scheme for our older teachers who had already given years of their lives to its work. Within the classes, too, there were a number of dedicated members who had attended for many years. Their loyalty was much valued and they often formed the core of a successful centre; but returning from newly established classes abroad I realized the dangers of introversion and nostalgia for an organization now thirty years old.

I looked around to see what else was happening in the world of physical training. The Physical Education Colleges were still in the throes of their conversion from Ling to Laban; and the keep-fit movement also used the Laban method of training for its class members. The Medau Society, whose Director, Molly Braithwaite, had taught our students and with whom we had a warm link, was now well established with part-time training courses for its teachers and classes run under local authorities. And the practice of yoga was beginning to be popular.

Yoga classes were taught by both men and women; some well qualified, others not; some were English, some Indian. They adapted the ancient Eastern system for Western use, omitting the philosophic and mystic elements and concentrating on the physical exercises. I found yoga classes very interesting with their ancient knowledge of *asanas* (physical positions) that could deeply benefit the physique, if correctly taught and understood. I realized, when I attended a class for two years, how much my mother had drawn on this technique when evolving some of her basic exercises. But I found the purely individual approach of each person with their own mat, involved only in their own movements, limiting, and I missed a musical accompaniment and a creative element.

The field of dance was more creative and exciting. Modern dance had become a general title used for both the educational dance evolved by Laban and taught in the Physical Education Colleges and in schools, and the theatre dance emanating chiefly from Martha Graham in America, its roots going back to Isadora Duncan at the beginning of the century.

This theatre type of modern dance was soon to make inroads into the Laban system and even into the orthodox dance companies like the Royal Ballet and Ballet Rambert. It advocated freedom – no shoes, no restricting tutus, no rigidly held trunk, but rather movement emanating from the centre of the body in an impulse radiating outwards and involving the whole of the self, unconscious as well as conscious. It was expressive and emotional, dramatic and contemporary, its themes often dealing with personal and psychological conflicts. But, unlike Laban, it demanded a rigorous basic technique, comparable, though different, to that of ballet.

It had a hard time gaining recognition. Britain in the 1950s was oriented towards classical ballet, enjoying the superb presentations of the Royal Ballet at Covent Garden. Despite visiting American companies, the concept of modern dance theatre was not immediately popular. But the next decade, with its hippy cult of freedom, experimentation and individual expression, provided a more congenial climate. In the mid-1960s the London Contemporary Dance Theatre and School were established, based on the Martha Graham technique, and the Ballet Rambert changed its focus to that of modern dance. These developments filtered down to the average woman in the form of modern dance classes, which became available in dance studios throughout the country. They appealed to those who were looking for an artistic approach to body training; predominately the young, who had the necessary unselfconsciousness and stamina to benefit most from them.

The first two-year course at the Bagot Stack College ended in 1957, with eight teachers receiving their diplomas. I then took over from Joan Wilder as Principal and continued in this position for four years. Joan had established a carefully thought-out foundation and recruited a talented staff. I enlarged the syllabus to include ballet for basic technique, modern dance for expression and creative content, and ballroom dancing under the famous Josephine Bradley as an added qualification which might earn the teachers extra money later on. Their training in Medau work with clubs, balls and hoops was undertaken by Joan Jefferies, one of our experienced League teachers who had studied Medau and adapted it for use in League classes. The whole added up to a demanding course and the students had to work very hard full-time to absorb it. In addition to their practical subjects they also studied anatomy, physiology and kinesiology, the theory of teaching, voice production and public speaking, and the organization of a League centre.

I was happy to be teaching students again and I learnt a lot in the process. In Cape Town, Barbara and I had been free to develop our work as we chose. But now I was Principal of a college and had to prepare students for regular examinations on a detailed syllabus. This tightened up my technique, even if it limited my artistic abilities. What mattered most now was not my creativity but *theirs*. I found that the task of equipping them to be good teachers was a long-term one, needing thought, reflection and endurance as well as vitality and inspiration.

We worked hard together and at the end of two years nine new teachers emerged. On their diploma day, Professor M.L. Jacks, a League Council member as well as a former Director of Education at Oxford and Headmaster of Mill Hill School, said in his opening address, 'The Bagot Stack College is producing teachers who have been given a wide course not confined to mere physical education, but a course of liberal education based on the activities of the body. This deserves official recognition by the Ministry of Education and the local education authorities. We hope to get that recognition and we are taking such steps as we are able to in that direction.'

Eleven students enrolled for the next course lasting from

1959 to 1961. At the end of it they gave a sparkling display of health exercises, movement with ribbons, hoops and clubs, ballet, mime, choral speaking, modern dance and movement-and-music. Two of the students' own compositions were also included in the programme. I then handed over to Anne Lillis who became Principal for the next ten years. In addition to her League training, Anne was a member of the Society of Remedial Gymnasts, an associate member of the Imperial Society of Teachers of Dance, and had done stage training at the Royal Academy of Dramatic Art. I knew I was leaving the college in capable hands.

The courses continued throughout the 1960s under Anne's expert guidance, with Joan St Lo as tutor for health exercises, and Peggy St Lo as Bursar. Most of the students were recruited from League classes and two scholarships were awarded by various League centres for each course. The League work learnt by the students was continually updated by the St Los, who devised new sequences of exercises and movements for them, as well as for the main body of teachers and members.

A highpoint of their creative activity was reached when Peggy produced a ballet for the consecration of the new Coventry Cathedral in June 1962. This was performed by League members from the Midlands trained by their teacher, Kathleen Ward. They were the first women to dance in a cathedral for 500 years. Dressed in medieval costumes, they portrayed three states, anxiety, faith and joy, accompanied by the music of Johann Sebastian Bach. Peggy had chosen simple movements which fitted in with the impressive modern cathedral with its Graham Sutherland tapestry and John Piper window. 'These dedicated women' as the Provost called them, danced their 'offering for the people' with a conviction which touched the vast congregation. And I, sitting in one of the front pews, was moved to tears and thought how immensely proud my mother would have been of this occasion.

The regular influx of well-trained young teachers from the Bagot Stack College helped to expand the League and keep it up to date. Many of them are still active and several of them have undertaken teacher-training themselves, as well as giving health and happiness to hundreds of women since their student days.

For myself, the 1960s brought me much personal happiness. Both my sons went to Oxford and gained degrees. And in 1964 I was married again; this time to an Irishman called Brian Power, a barrister who lectured on public speaking (I quickly recruited his talents on one of our students' courses!), whose wit and irony proved a good contrast to my rose-tinted idealism. We lived in London and Sussex and spent our holidays in a croft house on a remote island in the Hebrides – an ideal place in which to work on the books which we both later wrote.

So a decade which had given Britain the Beatles, the pill, the hippies and student unrest came to an end. It had also produced fundamental changes in women's role in society. And now the League – experienced, consolidated, as active as ever – had to be ready to exploit them.

10

An Enduring Vision

The end of the 1960s saw two big new developments within the League, which would have delighted its founder. Both took advantage of the freedom, greater earning power and greater independence increasingly available to women.

The first was the inauguration of Overseas Conventions. League centres were flourishing in Canada, South Africa, Rhodesia,which had opened in 1964, and New Zealand.

Why not visit them? thought Elizabeth Mallett, one of the League's senior teachers. Why not take a plane-load of members overseas to be welcomed by their counterparts abroad?

Her own daughter, Sarah, was teaching for the League in Toronto. Elizabeth decided to start there. In the event, her enthusiasm and the members' response were so great that *three* plane-loads, each carrying over a hundred members, flew to Canada in May 1968. They were entertained and given hospitality by the Toronto members, took part in classes and a display, and saw something of Canada, visiting the Niagara Falls and the St Lawrence Thousand Islands. Four of them wrote afterwards, 'How fortunate we are to belong to an organization that provides friendliness the world over.'

This pioneer trip was followed by visits to Vancouver, South Africa, Rhodesia and New Zealand. All of these were so successful that Elizabeth then organized twice-yearly holidays abroad for members, as well as return trips to all the overseas League centres. She also took advantage of leisure holidays run by holiday camps in Britain and gained special terms for groups of members and their families, so that they could enjoy League classes and contacts as well as take part in the other sports and activities provided. During the 1970s and 1980s over a thousand women a year benefited from these holidays, and Elizabeth's vision and enterprise added a new dimension to the League's work.

The second new development was more controversial. For some time the League had been encouraged by official bodies to run a shorter teacher-training course. All its contemporaries – the Keep Fit Association, the Medau Society and the Margaret Morris Movement – trained their teachers part-time. Adult education, said the Department of Education and Science, did not warrant a full-time two-year diploma course. The Ministry gave recognition to the Physical Education Colleges which produced full-time teachers for schools but withheld it from the League which dealt with the adult population. So its teacher training had always to be financed entirely from its own resources.

League centres and members were very generous in their support of the Bagot Stack College and proud of the teachers it produced, but it became increasingly obvious that students could not be expected to bear the heavy expense of two years of training and accommodation in London when the financial rewards for their work afterwards were slim and other subsidized training courses were available on a part-time basis.

Another factor to consider was the keenness of many League members to become teachers in their own areas. If a part-time course was available, they would be able to make use of it and afterwards teach part-time from their homes. So many of the League's young teachers, trained in London, left their centres to marry or move elsewhere after only a few years' residence.

The Bagot Stack College possessed a special mystique for the teachers who had trained there; none of them, nor any of the older teachers who had accepted my mother's doctrine of 'only the best', wanted to see it close. Yet adaptation to present conditions was essential. At a teachers' meeting, in 1968, Marnel King, a former Principal of the Bagot Stack Health School, suggested that we should try a pilot part-time course to be run at the same time as the college training, and see what happened. This was agreed upon.

Marnel and I then visited the Central Council of Physical Recreation and with the help of Olive Newson, our liaison officer there, drew up a syllabus for a year's part-time course which she submitted to the Department of Education and Science. They approved of it and agreed to pay half the cost. We could go ahead.

Students were recruited in two areas – twenty-one in the Midlands and fourteen in the south-west. Joan Jefferies and Elizabeth Mallett, both very busy senior teachers but prepared to give this new venture a trial, were appointed as Course Directors. And in January 1969 the new type of training was launched. Just before it began Joan, Elizabeth and I had a drink together and, with some trepidation, toasted its success!

None of us could foresee how it would develop. My main concern was that it would not produce too great a rift between the old and the new; for many teachers felt threatened by it and disapproved. As Chairman of the Training Committee I tried to reassure them and hoped that good results would overcome prejudices. In my heart I felt sure that my mother would have welcomed this expansion of her work, which brought it within the range of those League members who had the ability and desire to teach but up to now had lacked the opportunity.

The standard set for the students was a high one. Most of them were young married women with homes and families to look after and often jobs to maintain. Their training had to be done in their spare time and they needed all their enthusiasm and dedication to complete the course. One year's full-time college syllabus was compressed into monthly day sessions with the Course Directors, three residential weekends, weekly private tuition with their own League teachers, and teaching practice at their League evening classes. Much burning of the midnight oil was also needed to master the anatomy, physiology and kinesiology which were essential knowledge for teachers of movement.

At the beginning of 1970 they had a final assessment, with Anne Lillis and Joan St Lo as examiners, and then qualified as associate teachers, working under the supervision of the League teachers who had recommended and helped to train them.

'How do they feel now?' I asked Joan Jefferies, when their certificates had been awarded.

'Wonderful!' she replied. 'Towards the end of the course we all agreed that if we'd known what it was going to be like we'd never have embarked on it! But now that it's over and we've got good results, we're very glad we did.' Within six months the new associate teachers had attracted 1,000 new members into the League.

In the summer of 1970 the Bagot Stack College closed. The full-time two-year training was no longer viable. The pioneer part-time course had proved that teacher training in different regions was the way forward. It would be partly subsidized by the Department of Education and Science and would give greater scope to teachers and members alike. The League Council decided to adopt it. We were sorry to forgo our link with Morley College, which had been such a valuable and rewarding one. But Denis Richards, its former Principal, who had been Chairman of the League Council since 1967, would keep us in touch.

The St Los and I were very sad to see the college close. It was, after all, the direct descendant of the Bagot Stack Health School where we had all three trained and into which my mother had poured so much of her enthusiasm. Many teachers felt that by abandoning the full-time training we would be lowering our standards. But I had seen the keenness of the associate teachers at first hand and watched the dedication of their Course Directors. I felt sure we could adapt the scheme to maintain and even improve on what had gone before.

In fact, the first associate teachers taught for two years and then received another year's intensive training, after which they were able to qualify as fully trained teacher-organizers capable of running their own centres without supervision. The danger of a two-tiered teacher system was avoided and full status for all was assured. Once established, this was the pattern that we followed for all future teacher training.

Before long it was being exported to League centres in Canada, South Africa and Eire. In Britain, thirteen training courses were run during the 1970s, including one each in Scotland and Wales; this continued throughout the 1980s, producing a constant stream of young teachers who could take over from the older teachers – many of whom were retiring after a lifetime of service to the League – and open new centres.

The League had succeeded in adapting its training system to contemporary conditions without diminishing its quality. The two-year part-time course was followed by a postgraduate year of specialized training, guided by succeeding Training Officers Joan Jefferies and Pat Rowlandson.

And what of the League members during these years? They were busy celebrating the League's fortieth birthday in 1970, its forty-fifth in 1975 and its fiftieth in 1980!

Celebration has always been important in people's lives. It gives them the chance to transcend everyday routine. Fiestas, birthdays, anniversaries, victories, even successful election results are all celebrated in appropriate style. The Church, with its fast-days and feast-days, kept a wise balance between self-denial and enjoyment. The Romans, in ensuring 'bread and circuses' for the populace, understood how important it was to provide entertainment. Even the Victorians on high days and holy days abandoned their puritan standards and had some fun.

My mother realized this and brought her members together each year for a great display that united and inspired them. We followed the same tradition, although in latter years the periods between national displays had grown longer. But a fortieth birthday *had* to be commemorated.

The celebration took the form of a weekend at Brighton organized by the London centre and the St Los. Altogether, 1,600 women attended. They took part in mass classes at the Metropole Hotel, invaded the promenade in their black-and-white exercise kit, and assembled for a mammoth banquet in the evening. The Mayor and Mayoress of Brighton, who came to watch my class, ended by joining in, sitting on the edge of the platform to point and stretch their feet. So did our guest of honour, the writer Godfrey Winn, who later addressed the members and delighted them by telling them that they were the salt of the earth and must never give up their health and beauty. (Many of them never have!)

The next celebration – the forty-fifth birthday in 1975 – took place in the Royal Albert Hall. Teams came from Canada, Eire, New Zealand, South Africa and Rhodesia, as well as from all parts of Britain. At the matinée the Keep Fit Association and the Medau Society each contributed an item, and the Junior League, comprising small children from two and a half to six, amused the audience with their unpredictable responses, followed by eight- to ten-year-olds who took themselves much more seriously and tried their hardest with good effect.

Children's classes had been run by the League since the earliest days. League teachers adapted the work to children's needs (just as my mother had done for myself, my cousin Drella and the St Los) and gained lasting results. Many child members grew up to be adult members, some even teachers, and a number enrolled their own children into the Junior League.

At the evening performance massed sequences of ninety-six members alternated with advanced work, and three overseas teams – Canada, South Africa and New Zealand – presented items, the Canadians from Vancouver dazzling the audience with a spectacular ribbon display whose taped music began with the sound of a champagne cork being popped!

The next day five hundred League Association members joined with all the overseas teams at a lunch at Quaglino's, in the heart of London's Mayfair, where they were entertained by the band of the Grenadier Guards in immaculate bright red uniforms, each armed with a brass instrument which they played at full volume.

The Canadian item alerted us to the fact that vital changes were taking place in the exercise world. Diana Kropinska, our teacher in Vancouver, had attended a number of dance seminars and workshops there and was evolving a technique which would lead from exercise to moving dance steps – springing, running and leaping. She used tape music and long ribbons that enhanced the quality of the movement and her girls wore bright blue silkskin leotards.

For several years many of our younger teachers had felt that a change both of name and of exercise kit was necessary to bring our image up to date. The word 'League' now sounded old-fashioned and the simple black-and-white uniform was dated in comparison with many of the glamorous leotards on the market. The Association members, however, who decided League policy at their Annual General Meetings, voted against change. A number of them had been members for several decades and were quite happy with things as they were. Some of the senior teachers also pointed out what the word 'League' had meant to my mother: a band of women pledged to an ideal. At one AGM they went to far as to consider a proposed new name, the 'Health and Beauty Movement', but the following year they rejected it.

The Canadians, however, *did* adopt the name and produced an even more exciting item for the next big event, which was the League's Jubilee Display at the Royal Albert Hall in 1980.

With 1,200 performers from 225 centres throughout Britain, 170 teachers, including 30 from abroad, 200 overseas members and a packed house drawn from a total League membership approaching 30,000, it was indeed a golden celebration.

Peggy and Joan St Lo produced it, with the help of their production team, and six of the twenty-one items shown were their sequences. The rest were the work of new choreographers. I composed an item called 'Tribute' in memory of my mother, which included two of her original sequences performed by 204 members who had joined in the 1930s and were still attending classes in sixty-five centres.

Soon after the show a teachers' refresher course was held and at it the three South African teachers who had travelled to Britain with their teams – Barbara Keys, Joy Flanaghan and Betty O'Donaghue – taught us some of their routines and gave us new ideas. And two years later, in 1982, Diana Kropinska came specially from Canada to attend, and inspired many of the young teachers with her vital work.

This was in line with the trend of the times, for during the early 1980s women who wanted fitness classes were turning more and more to dance. In June 1979 Debbie Moore opened her Pineapple Studio in Covent Garden, started initially for professional dancers in London's chorus lines, but soon attracting many young women who liked the fashionable exercise clothes and the taped pop music. In fact Pineapple, with its more commercial approach, made most of its money from its fashion range.

'It was clear in the late 1970s that something revolutionary was happening to leisure-wear,' said Debbie Moore. She exploited this trend. By 1982 the Pineapple Group was ready for a million pound stock market flotation. It had radically changed the look of fitness classes.

Commercial competition on this scale was something the League had never experienced before. The older teachers and members found it hard to accept. The idea of service to the community – giving something to it rather than demanding something from it – was fundamental to them, reinforced by the experience of war. Perhaps it could only be fully understood by those who had lived through that period. Would the League's sense of commitment and idealism have to be sacrificed in order to keep up with the times?

Pineapple was followed by the aerobic revolution that reached Britain a year later, in 1983, and proved a real threat to the League. It was imported from America where the film star Jane Fonda was its arch-priestess. Backed by big business firms who manufactured health foods, leisure-wear, books, videos and cassettes, aerobic classes sprang up everywhere, ranging from ones in £400-a-year health clubs to high street classes at £2 apiece. They were fast-moving, strenuous and very energetic. Pupils wore the latest dance clothes and learnt repetitive routines to loud tape music with a hypnotic beat. Teachers were mostly ex-dancers with good figures and good movement but little knowledge of the theory of teaching or of anatomy or physiology. They usually taught with their backs to their pupils, who followed as best they could. Before long, injuries of backs, feet and knees occurred.

The aerobic craze continued, nevertheless, and newly qualified League teachers found it very hard to start classes in competition without the same financial resources or glamorous image. Their work and outlook was quite different – gentler exercise, graded to suit the ability of the pupils, attention to individuals, encouragement of a group spirit, and the application of the theory they had learnt to the needs of the body. Many of the new teachers were absorbed into League centres already in being, but it was clear that a change of approach was necessary to start successful new classes for the young.

However, before tackling this problem, the League staged another event at the Royal Albert Hall: this time the commemoration of the centenary of its founder's birth in 1883. A rally and display brought members together from all parts of the country. It was preceded by a run around Hyde Park at the end of which the winner sprinted across the road, into the Albert Hall and up the centre of the arena to present me with a cheque for £6,000 for Cancer Research and Relief. This was the final offering to the Bagot Stack Centenary Fund set up the previous year by Seona Ross, one of our early teachers who had trained under my mother. The magnificent sum of £28,000 was subscribed by members throughout Britain and abroad as proof of the love and loyalty they still felt for the League's founder. It was given to the Stoke Mandeville Hospital where later a plaque, surmounted by Peggy's leaping figure in silver, with the words *Movement Is Life*, was erected in the Physiotherapy Room of the Spinal Injuries Unit to the memory of my mother.

Her work had by now embraced four generations – her own, mine, my children's and their children's – and its age-range varied from two and a half to eighty-five years or over. It had grown like a tree with spreading branches, among whose leaves nested different types of birds. Variety had stemmed from her original concept, as she would have wished it to do.

'My exercises are the basis, the jumping-off ground,' she used to tell me. 'From that basis people must go on to whatever suits them best – remedial healing, sport, dance, artistic movement, choreography. . . . '

One of the tests of the system was the number of older women who could still perform it. Many of them joined an organization called EXTEND – Exercise Training for the Elderly and Disabled – which had been started in 1967 by Penny Copple, one of the first part-time course teachers. A nurse herself, she had benefited greatly from the League training and now adapted it to patients in hospitals and retirement homes, to whom it brought new hope, as well as to elderly members of classes. She ran short courses for already qualified nurses, physiotherapists and physical training experts (both men and women) in the basic principles of the Bagot Stack system, and they carried these into their professions.

EXTEND continues to this day, supported by a grant from the Department of Health and Social Service and affiliated to the League, which has provided a number of its teachers and all its Course Directors. Eleven years after its inception it has trained 700 teachers who look after around 15,000 members in their classes and are doing work of real value among the nation's ageing community.

And what of the young element? At its inception, the League had been dominated by the young. I was seventeen when I started teaching, the St Los a few years older. Students were admitted for training at eighteen and became qualified teachers by twenty. In those days we all had the confidence of youth; no task was too hard for us.

As the years passed, teachers and members grew older together, many of them giving wonderful service and loyalty to the League. At the same time there was a steady influx of young teachers from the training courses. The need now was to bring on this new generation and to train them so that soon they could accept positions of responsibility and have a say in the future of the League.

A beginning was made in 1975 when several of them started to train as Course Directors. It was continued in 1982 when a group of young teachers, accompanied by four members, travelled to South Africa at the invitation of the South African League. Two of them, Margaret McAllister and Margaret Peggie, were chosen to compose a special item which the team performed at the Johannesburg centre's twenty-fifth birthday rally, the Pretoria centre's twenty-first, and in Cape Town.

'Sounds Scarlet' was the name the two Margarets chose for their item. They dressed it in bright red leotards and for music used a classic rock tape composed by Mick Jagger and played by the London Symphony Orchestra. Dramatic as its title, this item heralded a breakthrough. The South African centres also produced some attractive new work, particularly in Pretoria, where the show was held in the Pretoria State Theatre, the heart of Afrikanerdom. And the Cape, when we reached it, was as beautiful as ever, living up to my memories. The whole tour was a marked success.

The vitality it engendered was badly needed at home where the League was to experience several years of trial.

In September 1983 Peggy St Lo retired as Organizing Secretary and the League administration was transferred from her home to a central London office in Charing Cross Road, which was run by the Secretary to the Council, Peter Hutton, and his assistant. Her going left an irreplaceable gap. She and her sister Joan had given a lifetime of devotion to the League and had made a unique contribution to its development. Teachers had relied on her to pull together many diverse strands; to be a friend and mentor as well as someone they could always turn to and respect; and to insist on a tradition of excellence. In the new climate of commercial competition, the League had to change and adapt if it was to survive; but to lose Peggy at the same time as facing this challenge was a threat to its unity. She and Joan, who had retired from the London centre the previous year, were made Vice-Presidents of the League, and Peggy was elected on to the Council, on which Joan had already served.

The London office in Charing Cross Road soon became a centre for public interest and inquiries, and later led to the appointment of a Press Officer.

The following year a new exercise record, a cassette and a video were produced by Elizabeth Mallett and Lucy Martin, one of the young Course Directors; and by 1985 the key positions of Chairmen of the Training Committee, the Executive Committee, and the Teachers' Association Committee had all been handed over to the new generation of teachers.

I welcomed this development. For a number of years I had felt that younger teachers must be given scope, must train for and accept responsibility, and must ultimately guide the League, for its future would be in their hands. It was also essential that we should attract young members into the classes. The League had always encouraged a mixed-age membership, and the grading of classes into elementary, intermediate and advanced had made this possible. But as the years passed, the efficacy of its health training had meant that members could continue exercising well into their sixties and seventies. They were remarkably fit compared with most other women of their age. Obviously they did not want to give up their classes. But inevitably the teachers had to slow down the exercise routines to accommodate the older members, and the young women preferred something faster and more challenging.

I thought a lot about this problem and we discussed it at the Training Committee, of which I was then Chairman. The solution came from a group of young Course Directors, headed by Lucy Martin, a teacher in the Devon area. In 1986 she put forward a plan to run classes specially for girls in their teens and twenties, and for young mothers, providing crèches for their infants. The name Lucy chose for this venture was STYLE: Stretching, Toning, Young, Lively Exercise. Pupils would wear bright leotards and work to music with a good beat, but also have the advantage of League membership and fully qualified teachers.

The Council adopted Lucy's plan and ran a pilot course in the autumn of 1986. Today there are thirty STYLE classes throughout Britain and they will certainly increase. They have proved popular in all regions, particularly in Wales, Scotland, the south-west and the north. They have the approval of the Sports Council, which specially wants to encourage participation of young women in movement and dance.

Another important development has been a move towards greater regionalization. Regional Officers had existed for a number of years in the League but only in a voluntary capacity. In 1986 eleven were set up in England in areas aligned with the Sports Council's regions and, with the Council's enthusiastic support and financial help, were given the task of increasing the scope and membership of the League in their areas, for which they would receive a yearly fee. A similar arrangement later took place in Scotland and Wales. In this way it was hoped to cover some of the blank spaces on the map where League classes did not yet exist.

The pebble that my mother dropped into a pool in 1930 has produced ever widening circles. The pioneers were Marjorie Duncombe, who inspired so many early teachers, and Peggy and Joan St Lo, who maintained my mother's criterion of excellence and enlarged her work with new sequences. They were reinforced by a number of talented and devoted teachers who carried the League forward during the ensuing years. And now a new generation of teachers is taking over.

The loyal older teachers who have given many years of service to the League and the members who have made it a way of life, they too have extended the ripples. They are too numerous to mention by name, but their contribution endures. As the years have passed, there have been conflicts and disagreements, from time to time, inevitable in an organization nearly sixty years of age. Some teachers and members wished for change, others resisted it; some cherished traditions, others welcomed innovations. But by and large, they have respected one another even when their opinions differed, and the League as a whole has remained united.

Denis Richards, Chairman of the Council for twenty years, has kept it in touch with educational development and guided it with wisdom and tolerance. His patience and wit have been evident always, particularly at the Annual General Meetings, where successfully to control 400 vocal women requires a special art!

The League has remained in close touch with the Central Council of Physical Recreation, and now receives a sizeable and much appreciated grant each year from the Sports Council, at whose suggestion it recently changed its name to Health and Beauty Exercise for working and publicity purposes, although it is still registered under its original title of the Women's League of Health and Beauty.

What exists now of my mother's inspiration? Times have changed radically since 1930 and the League has changed with them. It started as a pioneering organization, one of the forces that paved the way for women's freedom and emancipation; it continued as a model of healthy living for many thousands of women; it weathered the storms of war and the readjustments of peace; and today it has embraced four generations of women and enhanced their image of themselves as free responsible individuals, well able to take their place beside men in a world of opportunity.

Its ideal of service has led it into the field of social responsibility, helping a number of its teachers to care for the mentally sick, the elderly and the disabled. At the opposite pole, its creative urge has attracted the young and given a spontaneous outlet to artistic talents usually available only to professionals.

Its spirit of friendliness has stretched across continents and will be evident once more at its Diamond Jubilee, to be celebrated in the Royal Albert Hall in April 1990.

Above all, perhaps, the theme of 'mother and daughter', begun by its founder, has flourished. The title *Mother and Daughter* she chose for the League's original magazine has been lived out by teachers and members alike. Starting with my mother and myself, it has continued through Elizabeth Mallett and her daughters Fiona and Sarah, both of whom trained as teachers; Jean Yuill, Course Director and Regional Officer for Scotland and her daughter Fiona, teaching in Ayr; Lucy Martin, Course Director in the south-west and her daughter Alexandra, teaching in Axminster and Chard and helping her mother promote STYLE classes; Margaret Peggie, present Chairman of the Training Committee, whose mother was a 1930s member; and a number of other students on training courses who were child members of the League or whose mothers, also members, encouraged them to train as teachers, or join as members.

We all know that inspiration can be immensely strong, and at the same time immensely fragile. It can shine like a beacon or be snuffed out like a candle in the dark. My mother's inspiration was the lodestar of my youth, and although at times it has wavered since (in particular when I have to deal with intractible problems on committees), it always returns when I am among the members at a class or a rally, close to the grass roots of the League. The human element, the women who need the exercise, who laugh and forget their worries, who are swept into another world of music and movement – they are the ones who renew me.

The League has maintained this inspiration for close on sixty years, which is surely a measure of its original strength. Its future, like all futures, is uncertain. We cannot foresee how it will adapt or change. But if it remembers its motto, *Movement Is*

Life, and preserves its spirit of service, it will prosper. Self-renewing like the phoenix, it will attract to its work those who can carry it on and make it valuable for generations yet to come. Women will always want to be healthy and beautiful. As long as the League can show them how, in an atmosphere of fun and friendliness, it will survive.

Envoi

I end this book in Lansdowne, the hill-station in India where I was born. I have come here with my son Iain to try to absorb something of the atmosphere of this place.

Together we climbed the winding road to the crest of the hill and saw the cantonment spread before us, enlarged now with new buildings and a massive parade-ground. The Gurkhas are no longer here, but Gahrwali officers looked after us hospitably, showing us their mess, little changed since my father's day, and some of the sahibs' bungalows still called by the names of their former owners.

I hear the bugle sounding reveille and in my mind's eye I see my parents walking in their garden, trekking through the hills, living out the two short years of their marriage. I imagine myself as a tiny baby held in my mother's arms as she watched my father riding off to the war. Neither of us was to see him again.

> But love is a durable fire
> In the mind ever burning;
> Never sick, never old, never dead
> From itself never turning.*

It seems to me that these words, which speak of her love for my father, also describe the inspiration which came to her for her work: the charge which she passed on to me.

* Sir Walter Raleigh, 'As You Came from the Holy Land'.

Much has happened since she was here – two wars, the growing up of three generations, the emerging of a totally different world. In it, her work continues. So I bring my book to a close where my life and my relationship with my mother started, here in Lansdowne where she first saw her enduring vision.